ITALIAN COUNTRY LIVING

ITALIAN COUNTRY LIVING

BY CATHERINE SABINO
PHOTOGRAPHS BY GUY BOUCHET
DESIGN BY PAUL HARDY

THAMES AND HUDSON

To the Sabino family, past, present, future

First published in Great Britain in 1988 by Thames and Hudson Ltd, London, by arrangement with Clarkson N. Potter, Inc., 225 Park Avenue South, New York, New York 10003, who published the book under the title *Italian Country*.

Printed and bound in Japan

ACKNOWLEDGMENTS

There are many people, both in Italy and the United States, I wish to thank for their interest, suggestions, enthusiasm, and help in making *Italian Country Living* a reality: First and foremost, Nancy Novogrod for giving tirelessly to this project, and for her unstinting support, superb editorial guidance, and patience; Carol Southern for her fine suggestions, particularly at the beginning of our shooting schedule, and for her help in Umbria; Gael Towey for meticulously overseeing the entire project; and Jonathan Fox for keeping us so organized. I am also especially grateful to Paul Hardy, for his wonderful design and for being such a delight to work with, and Guy Bouchet for taking so many splendid photographs. Gayle Benderoff and Deborah Geltman gave generously of their time to ensure the book proceeded smoothly and I'm particularly appreciative of their advice and encouragement.

In Italy many people went out of their way to make sure our stay was enjoyable and productive. My special thanks to Nives Gamberana, Giuliano Coppini during our shoots in Tuscany, Count Francesco Foroni Lo Faro for taking time one busy Sunday to show me several *case coloniche*, Anna Maria Madai Fodde for helping us get to know the Costa Smeralda, and Laura Bonaparte for putting us all together, Luigi Vietti and Savin Couëlle for making sure we saw so many houses, the late Count Giorgio Frigeri and his wife, Countess Marian Frigeri, for their hospitality in the Amalfi region, Lino Gamberana for looking after us while we were in Courmayeur, Massimo Feriani at the Cristallo for all his assistance in Cortina d'Ampezzo. Beppe Modenese, always efficient and helpful, made an enormous difference in Lake Como, as did Tita Brunetti, Ferdinando Antonini, Giovanni Patrini, Filippo Perego, Michele Canepa, and Licia Catelli. Renzo Mongiardino and Albert Ponus kindly shared their thoughts on the style of houses in the Italian countryside.

Robert Talignani at ENIT never tired of my endless questions and Enza Cirrincione at CIGA helped us to make our work in Cortina go smoothly. David Breul at *European Travel and Life* allowed me to go from one great assignment to the next when I wasn't working on the book.

One of the delights of this project was getting a chance to talk to old friends and make new ones. For their help over the last two years, I'd like to thank: Giancarlo Alhadeff, Hedy Giusti Allen, Logan Bentley, Bernard Bohn, Bianca Borletti, Ida Borletti, Momi and Simonetta Brandolini, Raimonda Caetani, Brando Crespi, the late Rudi Crespi, Linda Dannenberg, Jean Louis and Lynn Sutherland David, Fiammetta Fadda, Bona Frescobaldi, Fiamma Ferragamo, Wanda Ferragamo, Massimo Gargia, Theresa Ginori, Rita Iraghi, Giancarlo Lazio, Count Giovanni Foroni Lo Faro, Graziella Lonardi, Fioretta Panerai, Marina Pignatelli, Carol Manchester Pillay, Aldo and Piero Pinto, Bee MacGuire, Fern Malles, Silvia Mantegazza, Aimone Mantero, Riccardo and Maria Grazia Mantero, Ilaria Marzichi, Donatella Magnolfi, Gabriella Mariotti, John Mies, Francesco Milone, Nina Monastero, Mark Rutman, Frances and Joseph Sabino, Romano Sartore, Giuliano Scardigli, Enrico Scolari, Alessandro Spicaglia, Oliviero Toscani, and Bruno and Lina Venturi.

My thanks to Marlowe Goodson and Alain Briere at Paul Hardy Production Studio for their enthusiasm and hard work on the project, to Ann Cahn and Joan Denman in production at Potter for carefully checking this book in its final stages, and to Mardee Regan for carefully testing the recipes.

Finally, to Alan Mirken, Bruce Harris, Nancy Kahan, Sarah Wright, Phyllis Fleiss, and Barbara Marks at Crown—thanks for their support.

CONTENTS

INTRODUCTION

To the first-time traveler, Italy's treasures may seem to lie in her splendid cities, in her churches filled with mosaics and frescoes, and in her museums and galleries. But for many people who have come to know the peninsula better, Italy's most abundant riches lie in her varied countryside. Consider Tuscany and Umbria's gentle landscapes, where feathery cypresses, shimmering olive trees, and vineyards cover rolling, sepia-toned hills; or the mountains, the jagged and silvery southern Alps and the rosy Dolomite massifs, dotted with villages steeped in folklore and tradition. Then there is the Italian lake region, a seductive geographical blend of northern and southern Europe, where pine trees and Alpine vistas form a backdrop for palm-tree-lined quays, stately villas, and semitropical gardens. And there are such famous Mediterranean regions as the Riviera, the Amalfi coast, and the island of Sardinia, with their jewel-toned waters, pastel-tinted villages, and harrowing sea roads with glorious views. The Italian writer Giovanni Papini noted that his homeland had "woody vales like Scandinavia, heaths as in Scotland, orange-scented woods such as in Andalusia, serene hills covered with olive groves and vineyards like Greece . . . flowering woods like Japan . . ." among countless other delights.

This bounty of natural beauty makes Italy a potent lure for people from around the world, many of them frequent visitors. Italians, too, are enthusiastic travelers within their own country, and even Italian jet setters, who have safaried in Africa, sunbathed in the Seychelles, and trekked through Patagonia, feel that the most enchanting earthly treasures lie right in their own backyard. For an Italian, *"Andiamo in campagna,"* or "Let's go to the country," is one of the most delectable phrases that can be uttered. *La campagna* is an umbrella term, often used by Italians to describe anything outside a city's limits—islands and mainland beaches, as well as fields and woodlands.

The Italian countryside can easily be enjoyed whether one has a little or a lot of time or money. One can delight in an afternoon drive through Chianti country in Tuscany, or visit a medieval hill town in Umbria, relax for a weekend in a grand, old-world-style hotel overlooking a magnificent lake, spend the month of August exploring the rugged and fashionable aspects of Sardinia, or head to the Alps for a weekend of skiing on flawless slopes. For the artist, the Italian country-side can often serve as muse. Writers have claimed that words slipped more easily from their pens when in Italy. Painters declared their senses more highly sharpened and their impressions more vivid, and even Winston Churchill thought he painted better when vacationing in Italy's lake district.

The glories of the Italian countryside prompt thoughts of languorous sojourns. Sometimes foreign visitors elect to stay on for months. The English have been enthusiasts of Italy and all things Italian for the past several hundred years and during the 19th century began renting lake-side and seaside villas for lengthy summer holidays. After World War II, many English people bought farmhouses in Tuscany and took up permanent residence. More recently, an increasing number of Americans have purchased or rented houses in the central Italian country-side, as well as in Mediterranean resorts. The lake regions and Alpine towns such as Courmayeur and Cortina d'Ampezzo are still visited pre-dominantly by Italians and other Europeans.

Italians dream of owning a country place, and what once was the exclusive privilege of the rich and titled is now a realistic option for many. Until World War II only a handful of privileged Italians could afford a villa in the countryside. Postwar prosperity and land reformation acts allowed thousands to buy and restore houses in rural areas or by the sea. Small condominiums and unfinished farmhouses can still be purchased at reasonable prices. For those with larger budgets, there is a range of villas and chalets from which to choose, although it is becoming more and more difficult to find a spacious residence in certain areas. Government-run preservation groups prohibit new construction in desirable resort towns such as Portofino and Positano and strictly regulate the modification of existing structures.

The style of living in the Italian countryside is determined by locale. Also, architectural and decorating styles vary from region to region. A country house in Lake Como will be quite different in structure and decor from one in Tuscany or Umbria. The formality and graciousness of the northern lake regions is embodied in their stately, classically proportioned lakeside villas, delicate antique furnishings, and formal gardens. It is a lavish area, built by an Italian and European elite. One Milanese described an imposing villa he inherited from his grandfather and justified the taste for grandeur of an era: "They wanted the same standard of gracious living they enjoyed in town houses and city *palazzi*. They didn't want to experience any 'entry shock' when coming to the country for vacations."

Even today the lake area offers a white-glove approach to Italian country living, but there are some noticeable differences from the past. You're as likely to find children's toys and bicycles parked in a marble-floored salon as a gilt-edged console, the *signora* of the villa in place of a cook whipping up a plate of *risotto alla milanese*, and the owner of the house tending to the hydrangeas and bougainvillea by himself.

Most 19th-century seaside dwellings along the Riviera or the Amalfi coast are less grand than the villas in the lake region, but an old-world ambience also lingers in certain Mediterranean resort houses. A house in Portofino or Positano may have fine antiques, paintings, and rugs, or may be styled more casually with white canvas-covered sofas and chairs, locally handcrafted rugs, pillows, and bed coverings, brightly tiled floors, and rough stucco walls. This comfortable Mediterranean look is particularly popular in Sardinia.

Interior design style in Italy has traditionally taken its inspiration from an elite, which was titled, rich, or in the vanguard of architectural or industrial design. Italians have come late to the farmhouse look, but the current passion for restored farmhouses furnished with rustic pieces signals a new taste for a less sophisticated way of life. The nostalgia for rural life parallels the country design movements in other parts of the world and represents an interesting change in attitude. Now, instead of filling a Tuscan or Umbrian farmhouse with fine antiques, Italians opt for rough-hewn furniture, hand-carved wardrobes and chests, handmade wooden decorative objects, colorful majolica plates and pottery, stone walls, beamed ceilings, terra-cotta tiled floors even in living and dining areas, and eat-in kitchens. For most Italian families, the concept of eating in a kitchen is a revolutionary one. Italians—for all their love of cooking and family life—have always regarded the kitchen as a simple service room.

A bucolic country style also prevails in mountain resorts, although the look is dressed up considerably more than in Tuscany and Umbria. It seems as if the sight of thousands of acres of pure, white snow brings forth a latent and cheerful instinct to decorate. Mountain house decor, at its most fanciful, is sometimes referred to as *lo stile della nonna,* grandmother's style, because of the assortment of tufted furniture, lacy antimacassars, hand-painted cupboards, religious figurines, ceramic stoves, and romantic bedrooms.

Italians and foreigners who have country houses in Italy enjoy their homes all year round. But the Lombardy lakes are most popular in the spring when gardens are fragrant and gloriously colored. The Mediterranean seaside swings into action in late July and rocks with social activity until the early days of September. Farmhouse owners in Tuscany and Umbria make sure to be in residence for the wine harvest in early autumn. Italian Alpine resorts are cozy and inviting from the first snows in December to early April and booked solid during Christmas and *Carnevale.* Of course, you can enjoy Lake Como in the fall, Cortina d'Ampezzo in August, and Sardinia in the spring—it is a simple matter of choice—but in *Italian Country Living* each region is featured in the season favored by its inhabitants and frequent visitors.

Whether you are planning a short visit to Italy, renting a house for a summer-long sojourn, or reliving vacations you've enjoyed, *Italian Country Living* will serve as a point of departure. It is an evocation of the glorious Italian countryside, the style and vitality of its people, and the way life is lived there today.

PART I
THE COUNTRYSIDE IN AUTUMN
Tuscany and Umbria

The appeal of the central Italian landscape—its gentle brown hills sprinkled with stone farmhouses, long rows of cypresses, and fortressed hilltop cities that turn golden at sunset—is just as intense today as it was when Giovanni Boccaccio extolled its languorous splendor in the *Decameron.* Tuscany and Umbria's beauty has changed little over the centuries, so that one half expects to see knights on white horses traveling the country roads and Botticelli beauties drifting through the elaborate villa gardens. ● Writers and painters have always loved Tuscany and Umbria. They treasure the quiet isolation the regions offer and the opportunity to participate in a rural way of life that pays minimum attention to contemporary concerns. In recent years many Italians—the natives of Tuscan and Umbrian cities like Florence and Perugia, as well as Milan and Rome—have rented, bought, and restored houses in the central Italian countryside. The beauty and peacefulness of this area has even lured a number of Italians from their beloved Mediterranean beach resorts, some of which are now considered too crowded or too socially hectic. ● A visit to the countryside is a

tonic indeed. Weekend invitations are eagerly sought after and many houseguests become so enamored of the region that they end up as residents themselves. Entertaining is informal. Lunches and dinners of hearty Tuscan or Umbrian dishes, freshly baked bread, homemade olive oil, and wine are usually served al fresco. An excursion to historic regional towns like San Gimignano, Siena, or Todi, to pottery centers like Deruta and Gubbio, or to local antiques markets pleasantly fills a Saturday or Sunday afternoon.

● Tuscany and Umbria are particularly entrancing during September and October when summer-warm days slip into clear, cool evenings. It is the time of the *vendemmia*, or wine harvest, the most important annual event in the regions. During this period natives and those who claim part-time residence say it's hard to imagine that there is any more pleasurable place to be. ● The central Italian countryside is easily accessible by car from most major Italian cities. Tuscany is a 4½-hour drive from Milan, and parts of Umbria are only 1½ hours away from Rome.

COUNTRY VIEWS

Over two hundred years ago Goethe said that **Tuscany** still looks the way Italy ought to look. Today many parts of Tuscany appear the same as they did in Goethe's time, seemingly untouched by the demands this century has made on other parts of the peninsula. Of course, some intruders have marred the idyllic landscapes, but for the most part an excursion down a remote country path or a drive along the Via Chiantigiana or the twisting road that connects the towns of Poggibonzi and Montevarchi provides some of Tuscany's most tranquil views and summons visions of a gentler past.

In Tuscany the landscape charms with its majestic simplicity. Visual delights abound at every turn. Olive trees shine on sunny afternoons as if their leaves were made of mirror. Churches with marble facades bleached by the noon sun seem like snowy castles. Cypresses turn velvety black

In the Italian countryside, left, a rural way of life endures in a setting that has changed little over the past several hundred years. From left, top: terra-cotta roof tiles, pecorino cheeses, a farmhand outside his stone Tuscan farmhouse, a terra-cotta jug, a farmer's son greets the newest addition to the flock, the columns of the Minerva temple in Assisi, sheep grazing in Umbria, an Umbrian *palazzo*, and plump grapes at the time of the September wine harvest. The gentle hills of Tuscany, right, are covered with a light mist at sunset.

The healthy olive trees, left, are some of the few to have survived the devastatingly cold winter of 1985–86. It takes a minimum of five years before newly planted trees bear fruit, traditionally harvested in November and December of each year.

Dark sturdy cypresses, left, splice the afternoon light on a deserted country road in Tuscany. The medieval town of Orvieto, right, perched on a wide base of volcanic rock, is one of Umbria's most impressive sites. The 14th-century Gothic cathedral has a brilliant facade adorned with multicolored mosaics and marbles.

as the daylight fades. Even the cottony-thick morning and evening fog that settles between buildings and in valleys and forests adds a mystical quality to the landscape. It never completely obscures as the fogs do in Lombardy or in Venice.

The region has been called a perfect land, among the most privileged of the world in beauty. Hugged by the Appenines to the east and the Tyrrhenian Sea to the west, encompassing the former great city-states of Siena, Florence, Pisa, and Lucca, Tuscany is just the size of New Hampshire, but its artistic contributions have been immense. Writers Dante, Petrarch, Boccaccio, and Machiavelli were all native sons, as were the artists Giotto, Brunelleschi, Ghiberti, Donatello, Masaccio, Alberti, Cimabue, Simone Martini, Benozzo Gozzoli, Leonardo da Vinci, and Michelangelo.

Why so many extraordinarily talented Tuscans? Giorgio Vasari offered one explanation in his book *Lives of the Artists.* "He [God] saw that in the practice of these exalted disciplines and arts, the Tuscan genius has always been preeminent for the Tuscans have devoted to all the branches of art, more labour and study than all the other Italian peoples." The achievements of Tuscany during the Renaissance—the 15th to 17th centuries—can be rivaled only by ancient Greece.

Tuscany gave Italy its modern language. Although many Tuscans speak their mother tongue with a somewhat sibilant accent, *la lingua pura,* or the "purest" Italian, can be heard in Siena. Subtle differences in dialects still exist, particularly in the smallest villages of the countryside, as do rivalries between the old city-states. But today, most manifestations of civic pride are limited to the fierce partisanship of weekly soccer bouts, or boasting of the superiority of a local wine, the sublime flavor of a town's well-known dish, or the academic rigors of a city's *universitá.*

Despite ties to towns where their families have lived for hundreds of years, Tuscans are very much alike in their taste for restraint, measure, and serenely balanced proportions, whether it be in art, architecture, design, or even food —the food of Tuscany as well as the character of its people is the least complicated in all of Italy. This sense of elegant balance is derived from and nourished by the harmonious beauty of the Tuscan countryside.

Wide meadows, gentle pastures, neatly cultivated farmland, and thick woods filled with oak, chestnut, and pine trees cover the countryside of **Umbria.** Italy's only region that doesn't touch

the sea, Umbria has an abundance of rivers and lakes that decorate its landscape—most impressively at the Cascata delle Marmore, a dramatic cascade created by the Romans in 271 B.C. Lord Byron fell under the spell of the falls and wrote about them during his stay in Italy in the 19th century.

While Tuscany's glory days were the Renaissance, Umbria's golden era came during the late Middle Ages, from the 13th through the 15th centuries. The Umbrian landscape still wears signs of this greatness. Medieval monasteries and abbeys, and the ruins of castles and their lookout towers, are scattered throughout the countryside. Splendid Umbrian hill towns like Spoleto, Assisi, and Orvieto, with their imposing communal *palazzi,* Romanesque and Gothic cathedrals, cobblestoned streets, and rows of narrow town houses, are reminders of the medieval past. Local festivals reflect the entertainments popular in the Middle Ages: the *cantamaggi,* or spring celebrations, when villagers dress in medieval costumes; Passion plays during Lent; the *Corsa dei Ceri* (candle races) in Gubbio on May 15; and the preparation of the *tappeti fioriti,* or flowered carpets, in the streets of Spello during Corpus Christi day.

The best way to know Umbria is to discover it yourself. A wrong turn can yield the most revealing images of a region and a people who care little about the race of progress. A tiny hilltop town, whose name doesn't make the guidebook, and barely the map, offers no boutiques, restaurants, or cinemas, and closes up each day at noon, becoming as silent as the interior of the local church. Passageways an arm's length in width will never hear the rumble of an automobile, or with any luck, the irritating buzz of the Vespa.

When the village "reopens" at four, schoolchildren play in the small central piazza named grandiosely after Vittorio Emanuele or Cavour, the elderly sit in doorways catching up on the town gossip, and the village's women congregate at the local stream to hand-wash their laundry. Outside the walls of the Umbrian hill towns, farmers till the fields with plows pulled by sturdy white oxen, shepherds round up a fast-moving flock on the grounds of a faded country estate. Umbrians, even today, prefer a simple way of life and seem content to live as their ancestors did centuries before.

In the Chianti district of Tuscany, left, feathery cypresses surround a large stone *fattoria,* or farmhouse. For defense purposes during the Middle Ages, Tuscan and Umbrian cities often had to be built compactly within a circumference of walls; their narrow streets and passageways, right, provide an interesting contrast to the open rolling countryside.

LOCAL COLORS

The colors of the Italian countryside, a palette of earth browns, robust greens, and transparent blues, are enriched by the mutable light of Tuscany, as it changes from honey to amber to roseate. Tuscan light heightens the sienna, umber, and copper soils of the region, adds a special luster to the olive tree's shimmery greens, depth to the cypress's rich evergreen, and a watercolor limpidness to the blue sky.

The Tuscan countryside was a gracious element in the religious paintings of the *Quattrocento* artists Piero della Francesca, Masaccio, and Benozzo Gozzoli, and the humanistic frescoes of the *Cinquecento* masters Da Vinci, Michelangelo, and Raffaello. However, it was not until the mid-19th century that its elusive light helped inspire an entire artistic movement, that of the Macchiaioli painters. These artists—Giovanni Fattori, Giovanni Boldini, Silvestro Lega, and Telemaco Signorini—sought to capture the lyric charm of Tuscany's fields, gardens, and lakes in their landscapes. They filled their canvases with *macchia,* or spots, of the blended oil paints they believed would best evoke the colored lights of Tuscany. The *macchia* captured the complexities, harmonies, and occasional trompe l'oeil effects of this light.

To the south the landscape of Umbria is colored with a jewel-like intensity, its green fields from spring to early autumn emerald bright, its skies an even lapis lazuli, and its thick topaz evening light illuminating the numerous towns crowning the domed hills. Umbria offers a lusher, *più dolce,* countryside that is as memorably colored as Tuscany's is, although in a sharper, more intense way.

The browns, greens, and blues created by man in Tuscany and Umbria blend subtly with their surroundings. No hue is harsh, whether it be the ochre browns of stucco *palazzi* and stone villas, the crisp browns of the local breads, or the polished chestnut browns of old coffee-house boiserie. You find flat green and brown shutters flanking most every window and golden-green olive oil at table. Workers' uniforms are bachelor-button blue and most Tuscan and Umbrian *signore,* perhaps more traditional than their northern counterparts, have wardrobes filled with classic navy blue gabardine.

Viewed from afar, a Tuscan or Umbrian hill town looks like a multistoried city, far left. The earth-toned facades of the stucco buildings appear amber, or even pink, in the early-morning or late-afternoon light. Terra-cotta urns used to store olive oil on a farm in the Chianti, left, age to a rich chestnut hue. A freshly tilled field, right, surrounds a worker's stone hut in Umbria. Large green grape leaves are speckled with protective spray, inset.

THE WINE HARVEST

A visitor to the Tuscan countryside will on any given day in early autumn see the tranquil vineyards, their neat rows of vines trimming the hills like fancy stitchwork, suddenly blossom with activity. It's the time of the *vendemmia,* or harvest of grapes, a crucial period lasting only seven to ten days, when vines are plucked clean of their deep violet and translucent green grapes and the annual production of wine begins.

Very few Tuscans living in the countryside escape involvement with the *vendemmia;* vineyards are as prevalent as terra-cotta tiled roofs in this central part of Italy. Almost every property, regardless of how modest its size, has room for some grapevines. Local residents like to let a few barrels of home-picked grapes ferment over the winter, creating their own personal brand of a world-famous wine.

When a private vineyard is large, all family members from grade-schoolers to grandparents, aunts, cousins, and in-laws pitch in to help pick the vineyard bare during those pivotal few days when the grapes are finally mature. Neighbors are enlisted as well. Thanks for the work in your fields is usually given by returning the favor—often the next morning, as once the *vendemmia* starts, not a daylight hour is wasted—and by offering a hearty meal at dusk, when everyone involved with the day's long labors gathers round a huge outdoor table to toast the new vintage.

No one—big wine producer or small farmer—rests easily until the last vine has been cleared and the *vendemmia* is "in house." Although the Tuscan climate is generally temperate, rain or a cold snap during that crucial harvest week can wreak economic havoc for years to come. Or a long, hot dry spell, like the one experienced during the summer and fall of 1985, can cause a "premature" *vendemmia* in September (the usual date is around October 7), forcing everyone into the sun-baked fields two weeks ahead of schedule to beat the clock and the overripening of the grapes.

Wine production is one of the region's most important industries as well as its oldest. Tuscany's premier wine, Chianti, has been

The advent of the Fiat tractor, left, meant a quicker harvest, as freshly picked grapes could be quickly transported back to the *cantina* for processing. Large oak barrels, right, hold the Castellare di Castellina Chianti Classico, which will be ready for drinking three years after the grapes were picked. Four decades' worth of Chianti Classico vintages are stored in the Badia a Coltibuono *cantina*, below.

produced for more than two thousand years, although the Chianti we drink today, an *uvaggio,* or blend, of red and white grapes, was developed by wine lord Baron Bettino Ricasoli in the 19th century.

Seven distinct districts make up the Chianti area, and each yields a variety of grape with a slightly different taste. Wines are named after the areas where they are produced. Italy's most noted Chianti comes from the Classico region, which is supposed to have the best soil for growing Chianti grapes. This area also possesses some of Tuscany's most beautiful country roads, linking the pretty towns of Radda, Greve, Gaioli, Castelnuovo, and Castellina.

Chianti has come a long way since the days when the straw-wrapped flask represented the wine throughout the world. Today, it's no longer economically feasible to cover a flask in straw—the expense of the raw materials and labor are high enough to make the cost of the bottle exceed the price of the wine. Just as well: The straw flask symbolized a Chianti or Italian red wine that was picturesquely packaged, cheap, but not very good. It's appropriate that most Chiantis are now placed in the classic shouldered Bordeaux bottle, which is perfectly suited for storing and preserving the great vintages they now contain.

During the week of the *vendemmia,* farmhands spend long days in the vineyards, inset. At Giuliano Coppini's country estate near Florence, workers toast the new vintage during the traditional repast served on the last day of the wine harvest.

17

THE ARTISAN TRADITION

From colorful glazed clay pottery to hand-knitted sweaters, finely crafted furniture, and even thick lace tablecloths, the handicrafts of Tuscany and Umbria are among the most varied and accomplished in all of Italy. Brashly painted majolica decorated with cherubs, arabesque designs, and mythic and religious scenes, has been produced in the regions for centuries. Less intricate floral-patterned ceramics in intense yellows, greens, and blues —the sort that can be found in most Tuscan and Umbrian kitchens—are also locally made. In towns like Gubbio, Deruta, and Gualdo Tadino, there are many small factories and shops devoted exclusively to the production and sale of pottery. Craftsmen will sometimes involve the shopper in the design process—the firm Grazia in Deruta is noted for this—and mix colors and patterns at a customer's request.

A drive through a Tuscan or Umbrian village often affords some curious sights as native women practice the crafts for which they are known. Seated in an open doorway with their backs to the road so that natural light can illuminate their work, the women hunch over knitting needles and embroidered cloth, samples of their finished work piled high beside them. The production of hand-knit sweaters, including some styled by well-known designers, has grown into a flourishing cottage industry.

The many wood crafts of Umbria, from cabinetmaking and fur-

Throughout the Italian countryside, small shops and factories produce fanciful ceramics, with decorative patterns often varying from town to town. An artisan, below left, adds a few finishing touches to the pitcher he has shaped on the potter's wheel. Artisans at Ceramiche Leona in Anselmo, Tuscany, below and inset above right, reproduce antique designs on plates and urns covered with white glaze.

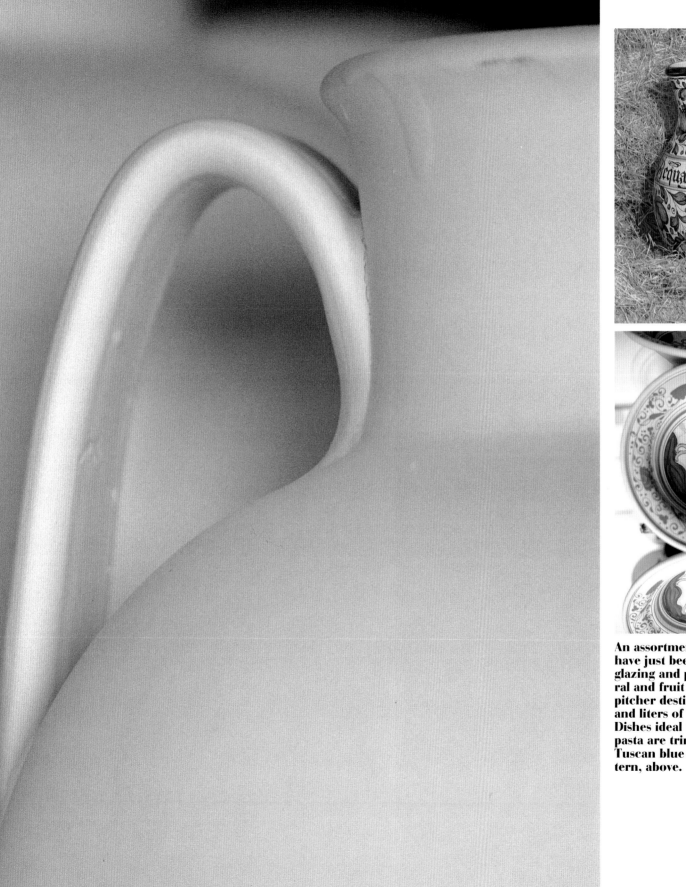

An assortment of pitchers that have just been baked, left, awaits glazing and painting. A lively floral and fruit motif covers a glazed pitcher destined to serve liters and liters of Chianti Classico, top. Dishes ideal for serving soup or pasta are trimmed in a classic Tuscan blue and white scroll pattern, above.

niture restoring to instrument and doll making, are supplied by the region's forests. The work of Orvieto's Gualviero Michelangeli offers a fine example of the blending of experiment and tradition in today's wood craftsmanship. A fifth-generation Orvietan carpenter, Michelangeli creates large surreal wood environment-sculptures, which have influenced the interior design of most Orvieto shops. But his atelier also produces a collection of wooden toys, rocking horses and chairs, dolls, and marionettes that have a turn-of-the-century charm and strong present-day appeal.

The lakes in Umbria are centers for crafts activity, especially along the shores of the large Lago di Trasimeno, where Hannibal defeated the Romans. Contemporary artisans produce thick laces for curtains, bed coverings, and tablecloths, as well as fishing nets and sturdy matting made from the stalks of cane cut down in nearby fields.

Shirley Caracciolo and a local knitter, above, bring the unfinished sweater outdoors to check the pattern and colors in the sunlight.

The rocking horse, right, wooden dolls, inset far right, and other toys created by Orvieto's well-known wood artisan, Gualviero Michelangeli, are among the most beautiful you'll find anywhere in Italy. The dolls are a reinterpretation of the *bambola povera*, which was traditionally made from leftover materials and old buttons.

At her home-based workshop near Todi, below, American-born Shirley Caracciolo finishes one of the sweaters from the annual collection she makes with a small group of Umbrian artisans.

THE FOOD OF TUSCANY AND UMBRIA

The cooking of Tuscany and Umbria relies on fresh ingredients prepared in simple ways. You won't find intricate sauces and gravies in Tuscan and Umbrian food, the formula always being less is more. The bounty of the lush vineyards, groves of olive trees, abundant vegetable and herb gardens, and hillsides dotted with grazing cattle is prepared with little fuss but maximum flavor. For example, the famous Tuscan meat dish *bistecca alla fiorentina* is actually just a particular cut of meat from beef raised in the Val di Chiana cooked on a grill over glowing embers, sometimes with the addition of olive oil and freshly ground black pepper.

In central Italy, bread-based dishes frequently substitute for pasta courses. *Panzanella* and *ribollita,* peasant bread and vegetable soups that have been made in the region for hundreds of years, are still great favorites, particularly during early autumn when there is an abundance of fresh tomatoes and herbs. Beans are another staple in many of the regions' dishes—whether they are added to soups, or to pasta for *pasta e fagioli;* cooked with tomatoes, sage, and garlic; or preserved in oil.

Tuscan bread has been saltless for several hundred years, ever since the thrifty local residents refused to pay a tax on salt imposed by the government. Toasted and brushed with olive oil, it makes a tasty snack, or when topped with tomatoes, a delicious appetizer. Mild local pecorino cheeses, bread, and a new Chianti are an ideal light lunch.

Although Tuscans and Umbrians do not have a highly developed sweet tooth, such treats as *panforte,* the dense cake made with nuts and spices and topped with powdered sugar, *pinocchiate,* small tarts with pine nuts, and *biscotti di Prato,* hard nut cookies, are popular accompaniments to a glass of sweet *vin santo.*

A platter of fresh *prosciutto crudo*, ham that has been salted and air-dried, and thin slices of *soprassata* sausage are served as a light appetizer at the Badia a Coltibuono restaurant in Gaiole in Chianti.

the ropes of dough on the prepared baking sheet, about 2 inches apart. Brush each rope with the egg yolk wash.

Bake for 30 minutes, until lightly browned. Remove from the oven and slice the strips on the diagonal into 1-inch pieces. Return the *biscotti* to the oven and bake for about 10 minutes, or until golden brown.

Makes about 2 dozen

SUGO DI POMODORO

Tomato Sauce

1 celery rib, finely chopped
3 to 4 medium carrots, finely chopped
3 tablespoons olive oil
4 pounds ripe tomatoes, peeled, seeded, and chopped
1 fresh basil leaf
2 teaspoons salt

In a large nonaluminum skillet or saucepan, sauté the celery and carrots in the olive oil until soft, about 5 minutes.

Push the tomatoes through a fine sieve. Add the tomatoes, basil, and salt to the celery and carrots and cook, stirring occasionally, over moderately low heat for 25 to 30 minutes.

Remove the basil leaf from the sauce and serve hot.

Makes about 1 quart

Preserves made from fresh tomatoes at the end of the summer are stored in an *acqua minerale* bottle for consumption at a later date, top. Crunchy *biscotti*, above, are often eaten with *vin santo*, a sweet sherrylike wine.

BISCOTTI

Nut Cookies

2½ cups all-purpose flour
6 ounces toasted almonds or hazelnuts, finely chopped
1 cup sugar
2 whole eggs
   Pinch of salt
1 teaspoon baking soda
1 beaten egg yolk, for wash

Preheat the oven to 350°F. Lightly butter a baking sheet.

Place the flour in a mound on a pastry board or table. Make a well in the center. Combine the almonds, sugar, whole eggs, egg yolk, salt, and baking soda in the well and mix together with your fingers. Slowly mix in the flour a little at a time. Knead the dough until smooth.

Divide the dough into 4 pieces. Roll each piece into a long rope about ½ inch in diameter. Place

FAGIOLI ALL'UCCELLETTO

Bean Salad

Beans: 1 to 2 ounces dried
  cannellini, Great Northern, or
  other white beans
1 tablespoon olive oil
5 fresh sage leaves

Salad
  4 garlic cloves, peeled
  5 fresh sage leaves
  2 tablespoons olive oil
  2 large ripe tomatoes, peeled,
    seeded, and chopped
    Salt

Prepare the beans: Cover the
beans with cold water and let
soak overnight. Drain.

Preheat the oven to 350°F. In a
nonaluminum pan, combine the
beans, oil, and sage. (Do not
add salt; it will toughen the
beans.) Add cold water to cover
by at least ½ inch. Cover pan
and bake for 1½ hours, until
most of the liquid is absorbed.

Make the salad: In a nonaluminum skillet, gently sauté the
garlic and sage leaves in the
olive oil for 2 minutes. Add to
the beans. Then add tomatoes
and salt to taste and cook for 10
minutes, without browning.
Serve at once.

Serves 4

**For *fagioli all'uccelletto*, left, the
beans are cooked with sage, an
herb also used to season *uccelli*,
or larks, during the hunting season. This is probably why the
popular Tuscan and Umbrian
bean dish eaten year-round was
given its slightly misleading name.**

BRUSCHETTA AL POMODORO

*Toasted Bread with
Chopped Tomatoes*

1 cup extra virgin olive oil
   Salt and pepper
4 thick slices Italian bread
4 large ripe tomatoes
1 cup minced fresh basil leaves
4 garlic cloves, minced

Preheat the oven to 425°F. Pour ¾ cup of the olive oil into a shallow dish. Season with salt and pepper. Dip each side of the bread in the oil to coat well.

Place the bread on a baking sheet and toast until crisp on both sides, about 15 minutes.

Peel and seed the tomatoes; chop into tiny pieces. Sprinkle with salt. Drain the tomatoes through a sieve. Place the tomatoes in a bowl and add ¾ cup basil, garlic, and remaining ¼ cup of olive oil.

Spread each slice of toasted bread with the chopped tomato mixture. Arrange on a large plate, garnish with remaining ⅓ cup fresh basil leaves, and serve.

Serves 4

The appetizer made with thick bread, olive oil, and tomatoes, right, is eaten in late summer and fall. It is called *fettunta* in Tuscany and *bruschetta* in Umbria.

A *minestra di pane*, above, simmers on a Tuscan cook's stove prior to a large meal that will celebrate the end of the wine harvest.

MINESTRA DI PANE

Bread Soup

This hearty soup is typically served after the wine harvest.

- **2 tablespoons olive oil**
- **3 celery ribs, finely chopped**
- **3 medium carrots, finely chopped**
- **2 large onions, finely chopped**
- **3 medium potatoes, peeled and cut into fine dice**
- **Small bunch of parsley, finely chopped**
- **2 to 3 basil leaves, minced**
- **3 to 4 large fresh tomatoes, peeled, seeded, and chopped**
- **1 small head of cabbage, cored and finely shredded (about 4 cups)**
- **2 cans (19 ounces each) cannellini beans, pushed through a sieve**
- **1 teaspoon salt**
- **2 to 3 small zucchini, chopped**
- **½ cup diced green beans**
- **4 cups beef stock or broth**

- **1 tablespoon chopped fresh thyme**
- **2 loaves day-old or toasted whole-wheat bread, sliced ½ inch thick**

In a large nonaluminum stockpot, heat the olive oil over moderate heat. Add the celery, carrots, onions, potatoes, parsley, and basil; sauté for 5 minutes. Add the tomatoes, cabbage, and cannellini beans. Season with salt. Cook for 5 minutes more.

Add the zucchini, green beans, and beef stock. Bring to a boil. Reduce the heat to low, cover, and simmer for 1½ hours. Stir in the thyme.

In a clear large nonaluminum stockpot, arrange some of the bread in a single layer. Ladle in enough of the soup to cover. Add a second layer of bread and more soup and continue layering until all of the ingredients are used.

Reheat the soup and serve hot. This dish makes an excellent leftover.

Serves 10 to 12

Panzanella, or bread salad, right, is a flavorful filling dish that is often served instead of pasta during the last days of summer.

Pane toscano, or Tuscan bread, above, is an important element in many of the region's dishes.

PANZANELLA

Bread Salad

- **½ pound (½ large loaf) stale or toasted hearty, crusty Italian bread**
- **2 large ripe tomatoes, peeled, seeded, and diced**
- **2 small red onions, minced**
- **⅓ cup black olives, pitted**
- **1 bunch basil leaves, stemmed and cut into thin strips**
- **3 ounces tuna fish packed in oil**
- **4 garlic cloves, chopped**
- **2 tablespoons red wine vinegar Salt and pepper**
- **⅓ cup olive oil**

Soak the bread in water to cover for a few minutes. Squeeze well. Crumble into a mixing bowl.

Add the tomatoes, onions, olives, basil, tuna, and garlic; toss together.

In a small bowl, whisk the vinegar with a pinch of salt and pepper until dissolved. Whisk in the olive oil. Pour over the salad and toss before serving.

Serves 4

A classic combination, locally made balsamic olive oil and vinegar, above, is the favorite salad dressing of most Italians in central Italy.

COUNTRY HOUSES, GARDENS, AND VINEYARDS

Tuscan and Umbrian country style today is best represented by the restored *case coloniche,* stone farmhouses, that can be found in great number throughout the central Italian countryside. Starting in the 1950s, the *casa colonica* was no longer the exclusive domain of the farmer. With the *mezzadria* or sharecropping system just abolished, 60,000 farmhouses came onto the market in Tuscany and Umbria as many farmers moved to villages and towns in search of salaried work.

A handful of medieval towers and even small castles have also been available for purchase in the Italian countryside, and despite their more august or historically notable pasts, these buildings are often in a state of greater disrepair than the average *casa colonica.* Some towers and castles have been completely empty for centuries; others have been used by farmers to house animals. In contrast, abbeys and monasteries in Tuscany and Umbria are usually well maintained. Religious orders have found these large dwellings expensive to keep up, and have sometimes sold them to local industrialists eager to convert the buildings into grand country houses. But while the tower, castle, and abbey can be made into interesting and often imposing homes, it is the farmhouse that is the archetypal central Italian country residence.

Case coloniche are predominantly block-shaped, covered with sloping roofs made of rounded terra-cotta tiles, and crowned with a *colombaia,* or dovecote, which sits like a little hat on the top of the house. The farmhouses are spacious, although they rarely have more than two floors. Most owners convert the former animal stalls on the first level into living, dining, and kitchen areas, and keep the bedrooms on the second floor.

The interiors of *case coloniche* have a rustic simplicity. Stone walls are left natural or covered with a rough layer of stucco. Ground-floor vaulted ceilings are usually painted white, and chestnut or oak beams supporting second-level ceilings receive a glossy coat of wax. The favorite floor covering is still the red *cotto,* a brick or terra-cotta tile.

Up until a decade or so ago, country homes were generally furnished with formal antiques or contemporary pieces; *mobili rustici,* the Italian term for rustic furniture, played little part in their decoration. But now rustic pieces from the 16th, 17th, and 18th centuries, like the large chestnut chests called *cassepanche* and Savonarola, Dante, and *sgabello* chairs, are eagerly sought after in antiques shops and at country fairs.

STUCCO FARMHOUSE NEAR FLORENCE

Even Florence can be a challenge to live in. Francesco Lo Faro, a native *Fiorentino,* and his family thought so; despite its beauty, the densely packed city has a noise level and traffic congestion that rival New York's. The Lo Faros wanted to move to the countryside, provided that the commute wouldn't be long—Mr. Lo Faro's work as a restaurateur meant daily trips to the city—and the cost too expensive.

Family friends in the small communities near Signa, a town about 20 minutes from Florence, let him know of houses that were on the market for rent and sale. A stucco farmhouse which had been restored 30 years ago seemed ideal: The property was small but peaceful, and while the house needed updating, the work could be accomplished with a reasonable budget. Francesco Lo Faro obtained a long-term lease and began his "readaptation," which involved adding new bathrooms, enlarging windows and

Although local preservation committees permit few alterations of old farmhouses, Francesco Lo Faro was able to enclose the original veranda and turn it into a second-floor study, left. Thick stone walls covered with plaster keep the house cool during the summer months.

Framed antique embroidered fabrics cover one wall in a guest bedroom, left. Marcella Lo Faro made the quilt and pillows, and covered them in fabric of her own design or in hand-embroidered cotton and linen purchased at thrift shops. The walnut headboard is probably a 19th-century Tuscan piece.

The blacksmith and his work area, crafted in wood, above, was once part of a large Nativity scene in Naples. An antique Tuscan *madia*, or bread bin, right, now serves as a little desk in the entrance hall. The small dolls belonged to a Tuscan farmer's family in the 19th century.

doors, and covering up a second-floor veranda to allow for a TV room and additional bedroom. To help minimize dampness, new *cotto* tiles were added to the floor and walls received a fresh layer of stucco.

Although their furnishing budget allowed for little more than an assortment of "finds," the Lo Faros have collected a delightful range of Tuscan and Piedmontese antiques. With an eye for the light and whimsical pieces, they achieved a very fresh interpretation of Tuscan country style. Marcella Lo Faro, whose small company, Sotto il Melo, or Under the Apple Tree, produces quilts, bed coverings, and pillowcases, designed all the brightly colored fabrics, many of them styled with naïf motifs.

"Tutti materiali poveri," says Francesco Lo Faro, all the materials are poor ones. But their artful combination has created one of the cheeriest houses in the central Italian countryside.

The original outdoor brick oven, right, where farmers who once lived in the Lo Faros' house cooked most of their meals, is sometimes used by the family for making pizzas as well as Tuscan bread.

32

A 19th-century canopied bed, right, was found in a nearby convent; the table where the Lo Faros' son, Luca, does his homework was purchased at a local flea market. The spare and simple kitchen, below right, includes an antique cupboard from Piedmont and a Tuscan table made from a local rectory. A small desk, above, from a farmer's house, is topped with a bunch of yellow *margherite*, or daisies, and a locally crafted doll and storage box.

An antique typographer's storage box now displays the Lo Faros' collection of porcelain figurines and marionette heads.

Cotto, the rough-hewn red bricks frequently used as flooring in Tuscan farmhouses, is left unadorned in the Lo Faros' small sitting room, above. The vaulted brick ceilings, right, serve as a reminder that the room was once an animal stall. A Tuscan kitchen cupboard now stores china. The wood pig was part of a carousel in the 1920s.

STONE HOUSE WITH 13TH-CENTURY TOWER

The stone farmhouse in Impruneta, a few kilometers from Florence, was purchased by Carlo del Bono, the owner of a jewelry shop on Florence's Ponte Vecchio, about 20 years ago. Without any architectural help, he and his wife converted the *casa colonica* and 13th-century tower originally standing on the site into a comfortable, spacious family home. They covered the interior stone walls with stucco and created an outdoor dining room by knocking down part of the stone facade; but whenever possible they retained preexisting elements: the thick creviced wood beams that make up the house's ceilings, the staircase of *pietra serena,* the classic gray limestone quarried in Tuscany, the stone fireplaces, including the one in the living room believed to date from the 14th century. The rustic farmhouse is the Del Bonos' primary residence, and they furnished it with fine antiques from their Florentine apartment, as well as with country pieces dating predominantly from the 17th and 18th centuries.

Like many Tuscan families, the Del Bonos gather each day at one o'clock for *pranzo,* or lunch—their son is finished with elementary school at midday, Carlo del Bono's shop in Florence is closed until three. A married daughter who lives nearby will often join them as well and help prepare such favorite dishes as *panzanella,* or Tuscan bread soup, *bistecca alla fiorentina,* and an assortment of fresh vegetables from their garden, all served with Chianti produced from their own vineyard. From early April to late September, the Del Bonos enjoy their lunch in the outdoor dining room. Overlooking a front lawn dotted with olive trees and an herb garden filled with sage, basil, mint, and thyme, this dining area is the Del Bonos' favorite part of the house.

The *casa colonica,* right, located in Impruneta, a rural town not far from Florence, used to belong to workers on the estate of a local marchese. The Del Bono family oversaw the complete restoration of the farmhouse and its adjacent granary, inset right, both of which had been severely damaged during World War II. Large olive trees, near right, grow past the entrance to the property.

Outside the *cantina* of the farm-house, Carlo del Bono, above, sips a Chianti produced from his small vineyard. The former granary, right, with its wrought-iron grille covering an opening that once helped aerate fodder, now serves as a guest house.

An impromptu drying room, right, was established behind one of the arches of the farmhouse's stone loggia. Freshly picked tomatoes, pears, and apples from the Del Bonos' garden fill the table. The fireplace, below right, in the farmhouse's central tower dates from the 13th century. An antique copper pot, originally used to heat water and cook polenta, still hangs beneath the wood mantelpiece.

A sturdy 18th-century Tuscan chest, top, stands in the entrance of the *casa colonica*. The Del Bonos—clockwise from the left, Daniela del Bono Andreoli, Giovanni, Carlo, Luisa, and son-in-law Neri Andreoli—enjoy noonday *pranzo* al fresco, above. The outdoor dining area leads to the formal dining room, right, which is furnished with 18th-century Tuscan pieces.

MEDIEVAL TOWER IN CHIANTI

Raymond Flower, the English author of history and travel books, came to the Chianti region of Tuscany on a magazine assignment more than 25 years ago and was so enchanted he decided to buy a house, even though his work kept him traveling to such distant spots as Singapore and Cairo a good part of the year. He became the first foreigner to settle in the heart of Chianti after World War II, pioneering the way for hundreds of other English people who have since bought and restored nearby residences. The region is so populated with the English now that the local Italians like to call it "Chiantishire."

In search of a place where he "could go and write peacefully for half the year," Flower chose an isolated medieval tower, part of which dates from A.D. 970. Once a lookout for the Florentines, it

The stone defense tower, left, built more than a thousand years ago, was destroyed and reconstructed numerous times over the centuries.

was destroyed by the Aragonese when they attacked Florence in 1456. Flower believes that the Florentines rebuilt the tower around 1460, when they were still in need of fortification in the area.

Most of Flower's restoration work took place in the buildings that flank the tower. One section, a former stall used by the farmers who had lived on the property, became a suite of rooms incorporating a small modern kitchen

Raymond Flower, English author and historian, above, spends spring, summer, and fall in Tuscany. A high stone wall, from which an entrance has been carved, links the tower with the former animal stable, right. Views from the tower cover miles of the Chianti region.

and a dining room, foyer, and informal living room. Across the central courtyard, another building, formerly used as a barn, was transformed into a library, formal living room, and solarium enclosing a pool. The medieval tower, complete with dungeon, remained basically untouched. "We had to redo some of the floors to reduce the dampness, and add modern bathrooms, but that was it," says Flower.

Furnishings were picked up at local auctions. "When I first came here, you could get a room's worth of pieces from the *Cinquecento* for 50,000 lire," he recalls with a certain wistfulness.

"And while antique Tuscan furniture isn't exactly the most comfortable, it was the best thing, in terms of appropriateness, for furnishing something like this. Anything delicate would have looked ridiculous, and modern pieces with their jujube bright colors wouldn't have worked either."

The Egyptian artifacts in a second-floor study, left, are the oldest objects in a very old house. Constructed with interlacing curved slats, the Savonarola chair is an excellent reproduction of a popular Renaissance piece. The Sienese tapestry, above, depicts the local countryside. Beneath the tapestry, a restored 17th-century *cassapanca*, or chest, holds an assortment of local wines.

"The splendid thing about this house is that it offers a lot of variety—you never can get bored with it. There's the pomp-and-circumstance feeling in some parts, Renaissance bedrooms, and monastic-like guest rooms in the dungeon, which by the way is the coolest area in summer, and the one that stays warm the longest in winter. The courtyard is ideal for easy get-togethers, al fresco dining, and I have numerous work areas, so I never can complain about feeling confined."

The majority of the time Flower spends in Tuscany is devoted to work, but he likes to entertain informally and frequently keeps in touch with fellow expatriates. He feels the region is particularly suitable to the English temperament. "There's a depth of tradition here in an ambience that's neither a social frenzy nor a void. Besides, the unxenophobic quality of the Tuscans makes you feel right at home. They're always willing to welcome today's invaders with a smile."

Flower moves a worktable to the pool area, right, during torrid summer months. The room used to be a storage place for hay. The stone washbasin, inset right, dates from Renaissance times. Located on the top floor of the tower, the master bedroom, inset far right, was once the quarters of the captain of the Florentine regiment that used the tower as a lookout in the Middle Ages. Most of the sturdy walnut furniture was purchased at the Arezzo flea market and dates from the 17th century.

CHIANTI CLASSICO WINE ESTATE

When Paolo Panerai, the editor of *Class*, a Milan-based style magazine, and his wife, Fioretta, a free-lance journalist, went looking for a weekend retreat in Tuscany, all they hoped to find was a tranquil, well-preserved house that could be inhabited immediately. Their busy schedules precluded the possibility of buying a place that required major work, and when they found the beautifully restored *casa colonica* in Castellare, they bought it on the spot.

Situated on a hill, the farmhouse affords a wide view of the Chianti Classico region, the wavy blue-black hills in the distance looking like the sea in certain afternoon light. The interior details of the house are pure Tuscan: white stucco walls, exposed beam ceilings, stone stairways, *vecchio cotto*, the classic deep red terra-cotta tile for floors. The *antiquariato povero*, or "poor" wood pieces of convents and monasteries, walnut *cassapanche*, decorative black wrought-iron furniture, and thick fabrics for curtains and bed- and seat-covers are also typical of the region. Fioretta Panerai sought to bring the colors of nature indoors. Bright yellow accents complement the fresh yellow flowers—the broom, sunflowers, and wild lemon-colored daisies—that cover the Tuscan countryside from early spring to midfall. For the dining room, fabrics were made to match the gray, white, and ochre colors of the stone exterior. In the living room, golden and red fabrics harmonize with the earth hues of the property. As with most restored Tuscan farmhouses, furnishings are minimal without looking spare.

The farmhouses in the Castellare section of the Chianti were built in the early 18th century, often with stones from the ruins of older monasteries and convents. The *casa colonica*, right, owned by Paolo and Fioretta Panerai, is surrounded by a garden where clusters of rosemary, lavender, jasmine, oleander, and iris grow among the rocks. A deep orange canvas reclining chair matches the rich terra-cotta tones of the planter, left.

The wine estate adjacent to the property had always intrigued Panerai, who couldn't resist finding out more about it when the 37-acre vineyard came up for sale. He invited Italy's noted wine expert, his friend Luigi Veronelli, down to take a look and consulted Maurizio Castelli, an oenologist. After a favorable verdict, he found himself buying all the land and instantly becoming a part-time winemaker.

"It was the perfect moment," says Panerai. "Chianti had reached its low point and was beginning to be revived. The estate had good if not great soil and was just the right size for the production I had in mind, about 100,000 bottles per year." Panerai applied his journalistic skills to his new wine estate, researching top wine production techniques throughout the world, visiting Emile Peynaud and Eric de Rothschild in France, and the Mondavi brothers in California. He hopes to adapt the best of the modern methods and is embarking on a cooperage project with Rothschild and Peynaud, which will enable him to bring in the special oak storage *barriques* that are reputedly essential for producing great wines.

With the aid of Maurizio Castelli, Panerai realized his first vintage in 1981. Today most of his production is devoted to Chianti Classico.

Even with a flourishing and demanding wine company in their backyard, the Panerais feel the Castellare home, where they spend their *ferragosto,* or August holidays, is extremely relaxing. For busy Milanese, perhaps the best getaways are those that require intense involvement.

Overlooking the Chianti countryside, the outdoor dining area, left, was placed under a grape arbor. A large swimming pool, above, was added in recent years. The arched stone loggia leads to guest rooms. The Panerais' vineyard, right, yields an abundant harvest.

Although Fioretta Panerai, left, her husband, and family live in Milan, they visit the Castellare farmhouse practically every weekend to oversee their wine estate. Nanni Gori, above, who manages the vineyard, is a sixth-generation Castellare farmer.

Wrought-iron window grilles and decorative objects such as candle-holders are frequently found in Tuscan houses.

In central Italy, bed headboards and baseboards are commonly made of wrought iron. The ones in the children's room, below, were crafted by artisans in Arezzo. Beamed ceilings, stucco walls, terra-cotta tile flooring, and the stone stairway, right, are typical elements in a Tuscan farmhouse. A bounty of wild yellow *margherite* adds color to the entrance hall.

VINTAGE MEDIEVAL ABBEY

Piero Stucchi Prinetti, a major producer of Chianti Classico, and his wife, Lorenza de Medici, a noted Italian author of cookbooks and a former fashion journalist, live and work in an abbey, complete with cloister and chapel, that dates from the Middle Ages. Located in Badia a Coltibuono (which means the Abbey of Good Cultivation) in the center of the Chianti Classico district in Tuscany, the property is considered a landmark, for it was here that the first cultivation of vines was recorded in the Chianti nearly a millennium ago.

An ancient abbey is imposing in size, and the Prinettis, like most Italians who have inherited a large home, sought to create a living zone where dimensions are human and appropriate for modern life. While the family's living

Now the home of the Prinetti family, the former abbey in the heart of the Chianti is flanked by a formal garden and small grape arbor. Historical sources show that the first vineyards of the upper Chianti were planted here.

54

quarters are limited to a string of rooms that open onto a formal garden, the Prinettis utilize the ample space that remains for work activities. The Badia a Coltibuono wine company which Stucchi Prinetti owns and manages is headquartered here, and Lorenza Prinetti decided that the house, with its enormous kitchen, was an ideal setting for a cooking school, which she now runs in the summer and early fall.

Mr. Prinetti inherited Badia a Coltibuono from his mother, whose family, the Giuntini, purchased the property from a branch of Benedictine monks in the early 1800s. While records indicate that an abbey was located on the site in A.D. 770, the compound's oldest remaining structure is the tower, constructed in the 12th century. The villa, once the monks' living quarters, was probably built during the Renaissance.

A school jacket belonging to one of the Prinettis' children is casually thrown over the corner of a studded Renaissance chair, above.

Sixteenth-century frescoes by the Florentine Mannerist painter Bernardino Pocetti decorate the living room's vaulted ceiling, left. Doors open to the formal garden. A small passageway, leading to an upper-floor study, stores the family's collection of antique books, above.

Both the monks and Stucchi Prinetti's maternal ancestors produced wine, but until recent times, it was generally sold to larger estates for bottling. Eager to distinguish the Badia a Coltibuono vintage, Mr. Prinetti bottles the wine himself, producing more than 500,000 units of Chianti Classico, white wine, *vin santo,* and the formidable *grappa* liquor, as well as honey and olive oil. The vineyards are now located several miles south of the villa in the small town of Monti.

Lorenza Prinetti centers her activities in the villa's antique kitchen, once a maze of tiny rooms that had been used for food storage. She conducts her limited-enrollment cooking classes here, offering students a broad sampling of favorite recipes from all over Italy. "I'm half Neapolitan, I married and lived in Milan and now in Tuscany, so I have a lot of different types of cuisine from which to draw upon," she says. But one thing

An arched window in the bell tower of the Badia a Coltibuono chapel frames the Chianti landscape.

Lorenza de Medici Prinetti, below, a noted Italian cook and cookbook author, readies an early autumn Tuscan buffet in her garden. The Carrara marble sink, right, dates from the time when the abbey was run by a religious order.

The grape arbor, above, is a reminder of the property's early days as a vineyard. Today the vineyards that produce Badia a Coltibuono Chianti span 3,000 acres and are located close to the Prinetti estate. An antique carriage and terra-cotta urn, left, stand in a corner of one of the old stables on the estate. A terra-cotta planter filled with flowers lies at the garden's edge, right, where the abbey's turreted tower is clearly in view.

the dishes have in common is ease and speed. "I don't believe you should spend more than an hour in preparation. Most often the best Italian food is the simplest."

When entertaining privately, the Prinettis like to take advantage of their garden—one of the most beautiful in the Chianti. The formal *giardino all'italiana* overlooks smooth Tuscan hills covered in pine and includes cooling grape arbors, formally trimmed box and yew trees, and stone patios embroidered with flowers. Beneath the garden is an antique *mola*, for stone-grinding the olives that produce the fine extra virgin olive oil which is such an important part of many Tuscan dishes.

The Prinettis have successfully turned their potential white elephant of a residence into a place that functions on both a personal and a professional level. They find the Chianti area at once relaxingly rustic and sophisticated. "It's an interesting place," Stucchi says. "There's this wild sort of beauty, a feeling of complete isolation, but the people who are your neighbors are like you, exiles from big cities, so there's a worldliness here that you won't find in other parts of the Italian countryside. It's a good mix."

HILLSIDE FARMHOUSE FROM THE 17TH CENTURY

Luca and Renee Mattioli, a newly married couple tired of Milan's relentless pace, decided to become urban exiles in the early 1980s, and live and raise their family-to-be in the countryside. Luca, a singer/songwriter, felt his career could be based anywhere, and for him there was no better "anywhere" than Tuscany, where he was born and raised.

With a "very limited budget" the Mattiolis scoured the Tuscan countryside for houses, which Renee describes as "a nightmarish process." Exhausted by countless false leads, she says she made up her mind to buy their current place even before she saw it. "The price was right and I just desperately wanted to end the search," she recalls. She didn't waiver in her decision when she finally saw the run-down farmhouse—"a shack, really, with

chickens running around. No one had lived here in 30 years."

The farmhouse, which dates from the 1600s, needed more than a complete overhaul—it needed digging out as well. "Since it's built on the hillside, whenever there was a heavy rain, a little more of the first level would get covered up. The work outdoors was as arduous as the work indoors," says Renee.

When Luca's professional commitments took him abroad, Renee proceeded with the restoration, overseeing local contractors and providing the finishing touches herself if the budget wouldn't allow for help.

To make the interior colors harmonize with the colors of the Tuscan countryside, Renee painted the stone walls with natural dyes. "The formula is a combination of terra-cotta and pink. I needed to get the timeless rosy

The stone walls of the farmhouse in Monte Merano were painted with pink-, sepia-, and terra-cotta-toned earth dyes, left. The 18th-century hand-painted commode is Venetian. Renee Mattioli stands in the door of her knitwear shop, right, located in the center of the medieval hill town. The compact farmhouse, above right, had been uninhabited for 30 years when the Mattiolis bought it. The lighting fixtures, far right, once graced the hall of a regional castle.

earth tones you find throughout the region." She also selected the slab of ecru travertine for the two bathrooms and fitted them each with unusual basins—one in terra-cotta found in a market in Rome, the other in marble that resembles a church's holy water font. After a two-year wait, the Mattiolis got permission from local preservation authorities to annex a small wing, which became a suite for guests—bedroom, bath, and study.

The house is small and furnished with "inherited things and flea market finds," which helped keep the project within budget. Once the renovation was reasonably close to completion, Renee began looking for new challenges —a search that led her to villagers who do piecework for knitwear manufacturers. She now has her own knitwear shop in the medieval hill town five minutes from her farmhouse.

The cotton pillowcase, left, trimmed with piping and crochetwork, was made in Tuscany. Knitwear-in-progress, for Renee's Maremma Maglia shop, is stored in an extra bedroom, above. The wardrobe was crafted in Provence in the 19th century. Noonday sun slips through the shuttered windows in the small guest room, right. The quilt is a family heirloom.

RESTORED FARMHOUSE AND WORKING FARM

Count François and Countess Shirley Caracciolo di Forino tried to find a little country house and ended up buying a farm. "The property was extraordinarily beautiful," says Shirley Caracciolo, an American who has lived in Italy all her married life, "and we instantly fell in love with Umbria." Monte Calvo, as the farm is called, included a large 17th-century stone farmhouse, a smaller house that was once a convent and was used during this century to store grain, a medieval chapel, and the ruins of an 11th-century tower.

"We were among the first non-Umbrians to live in the area," she recalls. "Fifteen years ago there were no major roads to this part of the countryside near Todi and it was difficult to get to. As a result, the restoration was a slow one." To oversee the restructuring, she moved to Monte Calvo with her young son, Roberto, living in the unfurnished farmhouse without electricity or heat. "Just the warmth of the fireplace for an entire winter!"

By the time restoration was complete, she says she knew she wanted to live in Todi year-round. The Caracciolos, who had once owned and managed a large farm in Puglia, the southern region of Italy on the Adriatic, moved from their Rome apartment and decided to turn their new property into a working vineyard and farm, where they could produce wine, olive oil, and cheese, cultivate vegetables and wheat, and raise sheep. Reviving the farm earned them the friendship of the local Umbrians. "They saw we were interested in the place for more than weekends, so they were willing to help us, even loaning us their farm machinery.

"Once the house was restored, I needed an occupation," she says. "I had always admired the knitting of the women in the region, so I designed a few sweaters. The workmanship was really pretty

The Umbrian farmhouse, left, was restored with materials from old buildings found in the region. The property also includes the Church of St. Blaze, right, which dates from 1050.

and we sold samples to well-known stores in New York immediately. I knew I could teach the women to do the type of work American boutiques and shops like, so with about 20 local knitters, I went into business." Today Shirley Caracciolo's sweater "studio" is located in a wing of the farmhouse, where she says, "I'll always produce something, whether it's sweaters, children's wear, or bedcovers, even if on a limited basis, just to keep the women employed."

The Arezzo flea market was the source for many of the regional antiques used to furnish the interior, including the five pairs of 18th-century wooden doors; there are also pieces from Naples and Normandy, which have been home to François Caracciolo's family. The result is an informal Franco-Italian country look. Bed canopies, bedcovers, and rugs were sewn and woven by local women, and floors were covered with earth-toned tiles.

The Caracciolos live casually, maintaining both the farm and the production of their elegant sweaters. Monte Calvo is a favorite spot for visiting American friends, who enjoy the tranquil, bucolic setting, fresh farm produce, and the Caracciolos' generous hospitality.

A former animal stall, the living room, above left, is filled with Italian, French, and English antiques. The sofa is covered with French fabric. Antique copper pots from Normandy hang above a travertine marble table in the kitchen, left. The large cupboard is also Norman. Terra-cotta floor tiles were made in Tuscany. The tall shuttered doors of the farmhouse's main floor open to a vine-covered terrace, right.

Count and Countess Caracciolo
sit on the terrace with the newest
additions to their flock.

One side of the *casa colonica*
was opened to create a partially
enclosed dining room, left, where
lunches and dinners can be enjoyed from April to October. The
Caracciolo family tree, graphi-
cally depicted on a large canvas
and hung in a small upstairs sitting room, right, reaches back to
the 14th century.

CASTLE AND TOWER IN TODI

Owned by the Opera Pia Cortese, a local charity, and formerly inhabited by farmers, the medieval tower and 16th-century castle near the Umbrian town of Todi wasn't for sale when Curtis Bill Pepper, the journalist, and his wife, Beverly, who is a sculptor, found it. However, the Peppers managed to convince the Opera to place the buildings up for auction, and outbidding their nearest competitor by $900, they became the owners of the Torre Olivola.

Beverly Pepper acted as architect for the restoration of the tower and castle, which began in 1973. She says she viewed the project as if it were a piece of art and slowly "sculpted" the interior, cutting into the four-foot-thick walls, replacing or lowering arches and carving out a gracious living area—winter and summer living rooms, a cozy dining room and large kitchen—in what had once been an animal stall.

Beverly and Curtis Bill Pepper restored the former Torre Olivola, near Todi, and its adjacent castle, left, which were built in the Middle Ages. Beverly Pepper says she will someday have the pool colored a gray-green to harmonize with the muted colors of the Umbrian landscape. Her abstract metal sculptures, right, fill one corner of the terrace.

She insisted that the local artisans she employed use only the measuring tools that were available during the Renaissance. "If the work was too perfect and calibrated to our standards, the place would have lost the sense of measure of its original period," she explains. She also required that the artisans use authentic materials. Stone, tiles, and beams dating from the 15th or 16th century were bought from local farmhouses that were about to be demolished.

Bunches of garlic and onions hang from a beam in the kitchen.

In the dining room, left, Beverly Pepper's sculpture contrasts with the refectory table and cupboard, farmhouse furniture believed to have been crafted in Umbria in the 17th century. Seasoned meat and game cooked *allo spiedo*, on a spit in the kitchen, right, are popular in Umbria.

A suite of bedrooms was created on the second and third level and a study for Curtis Pepper in the old tower. Windows were placed throughout to emphasize the graceful, Umbrian vistas. While the house had to be supplied with electricity and phone lines, the Peppers made sure that all wires were hidden underground "to leave the countryside as it always has been."

Curtis Pepper oversaw the landscaping and painstakingly restored the terrace with stones from Todi's main piazza. A few hundred meters from the walled compound is the studio where Beverly Pepper works on her large, natural-material sculptures. "I like to do my main work here, rather than in New York where I also maintain a studio. I'm surrounded by such beauty and can enjoy all the isolation I want, even though with each passing year we have more and more friends who have come to visit us, fallen in love with the place, and decided to buy nearby farmhouses and restore them like we did."

An Alexander Liberman painting and a Beverly Pepper sculpture are located at the entrance to the tower, above. Building materials from the 15th and 16th centuries were used in the restoration of the living room, with its vaulted stone ceiling, right. The walls of the former granary are 4 feet thick.

PART II

THE ITALIAN ALPS IN WINTER

Cortina d'Ampezzo and Courmayeur

Italians are as enthusiastic about *le montagne,* their mountains, as they are about the seaside. This often comes as a surprise to those visitors who think of Italy as a country where the Mediterranean climate colors most aspects of life. But rimming the top of the Italian peninsula in a gentle curve, from the French border in the West to Yugoslavia in the East, the Alps are a magnet for Italians from Venice to Sicily, who like to ski as frequently and for as long as they possibly can. ● On Friday nights in winter, northbound highways leading out of Milan, Turin, and Venice are jammed with compact Italian cars topped by ski equipment. ● Even the best-known resorts are virtually empty midweek when school is in session, but during school holidays—two or three weeks at Christmas, a midwinter break to coincide with *Carnevale* (the pre-Lenten celebration), and Easter week—Italian ski centers are booked solid. Since skiing in Italy is such a family affair, many Italians buy an apartment or a house near their favorite Alpine ski center. The

next best thing to owning a mountain house is staying in a resort's grand hotel, where guests are pampered in the old-world tradition and style. ● The Italian skier is nothing if not a bon vivant—you'll rarely see him on the slopes before

10 A.M., or when it's too windy or cold. A visit to the Italian Alps can be enjoyable even if you don't get near a pair of skis. The après-ski life is refined to an art, and as respectable an endeavor as conquering a dozen moguls. The parade of well-dressed would-be skiers through chic mountain villages begins early in the morning. In the late afternoon, villages fill up again with fashionable strollers, young men and women who eye one another with a mixture of interest and

detachment, and with skiers fresh from the slopes. By nine, a handful of restaurants become the rendezvous spots. The heartiest visitors may continue well into the early hours of the morning at some noisy, crowded discothèque or house party. ● While Italians have hundreds of ski centers from which to choose, the resorts that are always in demand are Italy's most stylish—Cortina, the site of the 1956 Olympics, and its oldest, Courmayeur, at the foot of Mont Blanc.

83

ALPINE VIEWS

Deep in the Ampezzo valley of the Dolomites, surrounded by forests of tall pine trees and fields covered in thick fresh snow, is **Cortina d'Ampezzo,** one of Italy's prettiest Alpine resorts, as well as its most sophisticated. Faded frescoes decorate the facades of buildings that line the village's snow-covered walkways and piazzas. Hotels in the heart of the town, converted from privately owned chalets, retain an old world Alpine flavor. Coffee shops so tiny that they hold only two tables are jammed with customers seduced by strudels, tarts, and pastries, as well as those in search of a warming cup of whipped-cream-topped coffee or a glass of mulled wine. Up-to-the-minute boutiques are a shopper's as well as browser's delight, displaying a splendid assortment of fine jewels, designer ski jumpsuits, and the cossack-style fur hats and oversized goatskin-hair boots that seem to be a perennial part of the Cortina wardrobe.

Snowstorms occur almost daily in many Alpine villages. Over a foot of snow tops a stone terrace in a house in Courmayeur, left. The Italian Alps include some of the highest peaks in Europe, quaint villages, frescoed building facades, and snow-covered streets, houses, and trees, right.

The official languages of the area are Italian and German, but in this town that attracts visitors from around the world, you are likely to hear at least four languages during any casual stroll. A Germanic influence survives from the centuries that Austria ruled many parts of the Dolomites and is still evident in certain customs, local dress, and cuisine.

Grand hotels were built at the turn of the century when the slopes were groomed for skiing, and the resort soon became a favorite of Europe's elite. Cortina has always had a tony quality, although since hosting the 1956 Olympics, it has expanded greatly and become available to a wider number of visitors.

Skiers delight in the many abundant cross-country runs in the area. You generally let the sun determine the course of your skiing, following it to the To-fane, which on uncloudy days are warmed with morning sunlight, and to the Faloria, which catches afternoon rays. There's even a ski jump—but that's the exclusive domain of the daring champions who compete on the international ski circuit. Cortina is a place where the finer points of fashion are meticulously observed by skiers who are serious about their sport—here candidates for the best-dressed list ski as fast as Olympic hopefuls. Many women in Cortina conquer the slopes in lavishly fur-trimmed ski jackets and precious earrings, rings, and a necklace or two, no matter how cold diamonds and emeralds get.

But not everyone feels compelled to ski in Cortina. Dressing well, getting a healthy tan, having lunch at Meloncino, the always-in-demand restaurant at the base of the Socrepes slope, meeting for drinks in the late afternoon at the Enoteca, the local wine bar, or the De la Poste or Cristallo hotels, and attending parties during the holiday season in nearby villas are as sporting as the activities get for many.

Cortina is delightful at Christmas when the slopes are filled with families of skiers and the town is decorated in red, green, and gold. It is a visual treat everywhere, and well worth a visit.

Located at the base of Europe's highest mountain, Mont Blanc—or as the Italians call it, Monte Bianco—**Courmayeur** is the most challenging ski resort in Italy. As you travel toward the Alps in the Valle d'Aosta, past snug villages, churches with bell towers, and the ruins of medieval castles, the landscape becomes rougher. Gentle hills and small valleys formed by tributaries give way to craggy mountains, plunging ravines, tumbling glaciers, and waterfalls that freeze to silence in winter. Clouds seem firmly connected to the sky in the lower parts of the valley, but appear to be scratched loose by the tall mountain peaks, settling below their summits like mounds of cotton. Stalky pines climb up

The heart of Cortina d'Ampezzo, left, has retained its Alpine flavor, despite the resort's international fame and considerable development. Grand hotels in mountain resorts have attracted Europe's elite for more than half a century. At the Cristallo, below, two guests enjoy the bright late-January sun. The view, right, is what one sees from a cable car traveling up Mont Blanc.

mountain slopes and give a furry covering to parts of the Alps and provide hideouts for the chamois that roam at high altitudes.

Courmayeur, the Aosta Valley's most famous town, has been popular since the 17th century when it was frequented by European nobles for its water cures. Today, it is a pleasant village, despite considerable development since the Mont Blanc tunnel, carved beneath the mammoth mountain, was opened in 1967. Like most towns in the Valle d'Aosta, Courmayeur has a French flavor and you're as likely to hear French spoken as Italian.

While the town has expanded and been updated since the opening of the tunnel, it hasn't lost its charm. A single carless pathway runs through Courmayeur's center, which is lined with boutiques offering classical, well-made clothing, bread and bakery shops with tempting window displays, small restaurants, hotels, and

real-estate offices. Courmayeur is as sophisticated as most Italian ski resorts, but après-ski life is low key and dress tends to be an understated variety of chic.

The people of Courmayeur are largely local professionals whose livelihood depends on the ski industry, and the thousands of visitors who come each year. They regard the mighty mountains with a respectful nonchalance, and will drive about in blizzards, expertly negotiating winding, icy roads, and willingly offer advice to the newcomer.

For a well-known mountain resort, Courmayeur is unusual, because its residential districts are inhabited year-round, and most of its grand villas are owned by natives. As a result, it's never a ghost town when the peak season is over.

The houses and buildings in mountain villages are usually clustered together. In the past being close to one's neighbors was essential for survival in a severe winter climate. Today, building new structures on virgin terrain is often prohibited, so houses are densely packed in areas already zoned for residential dwellings.

LOCAL COLORS

The day after a snowstorm in the Italian Alps, hills and fields look as if they've been covered in thick white cream and sprinkled with glittering sugar crystals. The white of fresh snow can have a blue cast, dazzle like silver, or glisten with an almost blinding intensity on sunny days, be tinted with pink or amber at sunrise and sunset, or appear a muted dove gray when the sky is overcast. Snow works magic on the Alpine countryside, making even the simplest landscape seem like an elegant silverpoint sketch.

Against snowy whites, deep pine greens, and the blue of the sky, the seasoned wood tones of chalets seem more intense. Even Alpine food appears to be colored to perfection. Rich yellow fondues, golden strudels, deep red *carpacci,* dark brown breads, and cinnamon- or chocolate-topped *cappuccini* tempt the palate and are as luscious to look at as they are to eat.

Italian Alpine fashion is known for its color and flair. Vacationers destined for chic ski resorts pack their suitcases to a nearly impossible-to-close fullness and grace the slopes in a candy-store assortment of pastel and lollipop-bright ski suits, sweaters, and leg warmers, adding a riot of colors to the snowy hills.

With a dusting of new snow, a Valdostano landscape looks even more delightful, left. Vividly toned ski suits and the pink light of dawn and sunset, insets, as well as a bright red cable car, right, add color to the white of the Alpine winter.

91

SKIING

The southernmost mountains in the Alpine range, the Italian Alps offer an abundance of sunny days and temperatures that are considerably milder than those at resorts in nearby countries. As early as February in certain Italian ski centers, you can slalom down the *piste*, the Italian term for ski runs, without a jacket or sweater. Besides good weather, Italy has kilometers of groomed slopes, and trails that can keep every type of skier happy, whether he is a daredevil downhiller, a hesitant novice, or a cross-country fan. Frequent snowfalls guarantee a long season, typically lasting from December to April, and trails that are always covered with a thick base of snow.

Skiing on the Italian side of the Alps will generally be less expensive than in Switzerland or France—in terms of both lift tickets and accommodations—and most visitors agree that the food in Italian Alpine towns is as much of an attraction as the slopes. Lunch in an Italian resort is a social happening; cable cars often shut down and ski runs are abandoned at one, the hour of *pranzo*, as skiers head to favorite restaurants right on the slopes or back in the villages.

An important point to keep in mind when you're skiing in Italy for the first time: Italians rate their runs with uncharacteristic understatement. An intermediate slope (red marker) can be quite difficult for those who customarily ski at that level. For example, the run from the top of the Tofane near Cortina has been widened and leveled and made easier since it was the site of the downhill race in the 1956 Olympics. It is recommended for good intermediates but would still be a challenge for most experts. Difficult slopes, designated by black markers, can be treacherous, and unmarked slopes, the most dangerous of all, due to an ever-present risk of avalanches.

Expert ski guides can take you through the most challenging terrain and are essential for certain runs, particularly in Courmayeur. A ski guide will escort you from the Punta Helbronner, halfway up Mont Blanc in July, down the Vallé Blanche and into Chamonix, France. Day and weekend excursions may be planned with the guides, as well as the weeklong Haute Route for accomplished skiers from Mont Blanc to the Matterhorn in Switzerland.

At the Punta Helbronner, the refuge near the top of Mont Blanc, right, a visitor can enjoy a 360-degree panorama of the Italian, Swiss, and French Alps. Ski instructors slalom through fresh snow on Mont Blanc, inset above right. A colorful label decorates windows of the Mont Blanc cable cars, inset below right.

THE CHEESE OF THE VALLE D'AOSTA

L ight, nutty, and slightly sweet in flavor, fontina is regarded as one of the great cheeses of the world. It is certainly Italy's premier mountain cheese. Fontina is as much a staple of regional recipes as pesto is on the Italian Riviera and tomato sauce is in Naples. It is used to season a variety of pasta and meat dishes, but the cheese is delicious savored on its own, preferably with a slice of Valdostano brown bread and a glass of local red wine.

Today the production of fontina is the major source of income for the region's dairy farmers, who supply the milk from which it is made. When traveling through the Valle d'Aosta in the early morning, you will often see farmers emptying cans of milk from

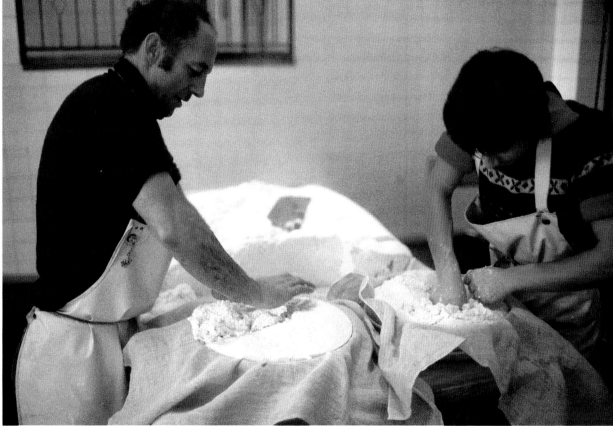

trucks lined up outside the local cooperatives where the fontina is manufactured. A visit to one of these cooperatives can usually be arranged through your hotel or a local restaurateur.

Although the cheesemaking equipment has a space-age modernity, the process is the same as it has been for hundreds of years. Huge caldrons heat the fresh milk to a certain temperature before rennet is added. Several hours later a pair of workers scoop out the rennet with cheesecloth. The warm crumbly mixture from the

Farmers bring cows' milk in metal containers each morning to the cooperative where it is weighed before being processed as cheese, above left. The warm milk curd, scooped from enormous vats, above, is kneaded into wooden disks prior to curing, left. The disks of fontina cheese, right, are set on large stone slabs in a milk cooperative's curing room.

caldrons is placed in large wooden molds, then set aside in cool rooms to age. The cheese can be sold three or four months later when it has a semihard consistency, and a light orange-brown rind.

A true fontina may be produced only in the Valle d'Aosta according to strict specifications set by the Consorzio Produttori Fontina regarding its fat content, shape, and size. Just about every food store in the region will carry the Consorzio's fontina, which is distinguished by a graphic white label. You can buy the cheese as a large disk, or in smaller wedges, the way most Valdostani do.

Fontina cheese is ready for consumption after three months' curing, but can be aged for two to three years in the cavelike storage rooms of the Cooperative Produttori Latte e Fontina near Courmayeur, left.

At the Cooperative Valdigne in Morgex, Armando Madini, one of its managers, stands with two workers, who proudly display a disk of precured fontina, left. The Cooperative produces between 20 and 60 of these disks each day. Butter, above, is also produced daily at the cooperative.

PAINTED FURNITURE

In the Veneto and the Alto Adige, the northern district of Italy that shares a border with Austria, country furniture is frequently decorated with lively motifs and painted in bright colors. This *arte povera,* or poor art embellishment, makes the commodes, wardrobes, and storage chests from these regions among the most decorative you'll see anywhere in Italy.

Arte povera evolved as an imitation of the japanning and Eastern lacquering techniques that were much in vogue in Venice and nearby areas in the 1700s. Venetian, Portuguese, and Dutch traders brought back lacquered furniture from the Far East in the 18th century, and Italian craftsmen studied and copied the methods that made the furniture so desirable. At first reproductions faithfully replicated intricate Eastern motifs. Gradually Venetian artisans became more inventive and used their own designs to embellish furniture. Craftsmen in mountain regions imitated their Venetian counterparts and began to decorate locally crafted furniture, often made from inexpensive cuts of wood.

In the mountain areas hand-painted designs and paper or thin wood appliqués, which were attached to the furniture after lacquering, were far less sophisticated than those found on Venetian pieces. Often religious or allegorical, the designs and appliqués have a naïf quality.

The commode, lacquered in red and adorned with elaborate scenes, was crafted in Venice in the 18th century, far left. The two *armadi*, or wardrobes, top and above, represent more humble versions of the lacquered and painted furniture popular in the Veneto and nearby mountain regions. The floral motif, left, was painted on the front panel of the 19th-century *armadio* from the Alto Adige, top.

MOUNTAIN FARE

Thick soups, hearty polentas, flavorful sauces, and rich fondues are just some of the tempting foods available in the Alpine regions in Italy. Over-the-mountain neighbors sometimes influence local dishes. For example, in the Valle d'Aosta, near France, it is easy to find onion soups, meat stews cooked in wine, and *marrons glacés*; while in the Dolomites, in northeastern Italy close to Austria, goulash, wurstel and sauerkraut, and strudel are often listed on restaurant menus.

A lunch or dinner in the mountains usually starts with a substantial first course—ravioli, tortelloni, or a local pasta, like the Dolomites *casunzei*, polenta, or *risotto*. Many of these *primi piatti* are topped with slices of the region's cheese, such as fontina in the Valle d'Aosta or Asiago in the Dolomites. Grilled game, and even grilled salad—*radicchio* and lettuce leaves brushed with oil—are popular second courses. For those who plan afternoons of vigorous skiing, or care to eat less heartily, chunks of beef or raw vegetables dipped in *bagna cauda*, a hot sauce of anchovies, oil, and garlic, or a sampling of dishes from an elaborate antipasto make an ideal light lunch.

A hearty antipasto prepared by the Maison de Filippo restaurant at the foot of Mont Blanc includes *tomini* with herbs, pepperoni, and zucchini flavored with *bagna cauda*, *prosciutto crudo*, assorted salamis, rice and bean salads, and *prosciutto cotto* served with boiled potatoes and cauliflower. For many, a sampling of these appetizers suffices as a full meal.

CASUNZEI

Ravioli, Cortina Style

PASTA

1½ cups all-purpose flour
2 egg yolks
1 tablespoon olive oil
2 tablespoons water

FILLING

3 heads *radicchio*
½ cup grated parmesan cheese
Salt

TOPPING

4 tablespoons unsalted butter
2 tablespoons poppy seeds

Make the pasta: Mound the flour on a work surface and press a hole in the center. Add the egg yolks, oil, and water. Mix the ingredients with your fingers, slowly incorporating the flour. Continue mixing until a sticky dough forms; if necessary, add up to 1 tablespoon more

water. Knead the dough until smooth and elastic.

Roll out the dough very thin. Using a 2-inch cutter or the rim of a glass, cut out as many circles of dough as possible.

Make the filling: Separate the *radicchio* leaves and wash well. Place in a nonaluminum skillet or saucepan. With the water that clings to the leaves, cover and cook over moderate heat until wilted and tender, about 4 minutes. Squeeze out as much liquid as possible; finely chop

the *radicchio*. Place in a bowl and stir in the parmesan, season with salt.

Place 1 teaspoon of the *radicchio* mixture on each circle of dough. Fold the circle into a half-moon shape and press the edges firmly to seal.

In a large pot of lightly salted boiling water, cook the filled pasta until al dente, about 15 minutes. Drain the *casunzei* and place in dish.

Meanwhile, heat the butter in a skillet. When golden brown, add the poppy seeds and sauté, stirring for about 1 minute. Pour the butter and seeds over the *casunzei* and sprinkle with additional grated parmesan.

Makes 10 servings as a first course or 6 to 8 as an entrée

Polenta, above, a popular first course in northern Italy that often takes the place of pasta, is also a staple in Alpine regions. In the Valle d'Aosta, its preparation varies from town to town. *Casunzei*, left, filled with *radicchio*, spinach, or beet root and flavored with poppy seeds and butter, is an unusual pasta found in Cortina d'Ampezzo.

POLENTA

1 tablespoon salt
2½ cups stone-ground yellow cornmeal

Bring 2 quarts of water in a large pot to a boil. Add the salt. Reduce the heat to low so the water is just at a simmer. Very gradually, stir in the cornmeal in a thin, steady stream, stirring with a large wooden spoon. Keep stirring mixture constantly for 20 to 30 minutes (if you don't stir constantly, polenta will be lumpy), until the po-

lenta begins to pull away from the side of the pot, or until the wooden spoon stands up by itself in the middle of the mixture. The finished polenta should have the consistency of mashed potatoes.

Pour the polenta onto a cutting board or platter, let cool a bit, and cut into squares. Serve with butter and parmesan cheese, or with tomato sauce.

Makes 6 servings as a first course

ZUPPA VALDOSTANA

Valle d'Aosta Onion Soup

- **1 onion**
- **2 tablespoons butter**
- **½ head of cauliflower, trimmed, with stems and florets cut into bite-size pieces**
- **6 slices whole-wheat Italian bread, toasted, about 1 inch thick**
- **2 ounces fontina cheese, finely diced or grated (about ¼ cup)**
- **8 cups meat stock or broth, boiling**
- **Nutmeg**

Preheat the oven to 300°F. In a large pot, lightly sauté the onion in the butter over moderate heat until just translucent. Add the cauliflower and sauté until somewhat soft.

In a large ovenproof earthenware bowl, layer the bread, fontina, and onion and cauliflower mixture. Pour the meat stock over the mixture and sprinkle with nutmeg.

Bake for 10 to 15 minutes, until bubbling and lightly browned.

Serves 4

Fontina is used in a wide variety of dishes in the Valle d'Aosta, like the *zuppa valdostana*, right, in which it is a main ingredient, or the spinach-filled *tortelloni alla valdostana*, above far right, where it serves as topping.

TORTELLONI ALLA VALDOSTANA

DOUGH

- ½ pound fresh spinach, or ½ package frozen spinach, thawed
- ¼ teaspoon salt
- 1¾ cups all-purpose flour
- 1 extra large egg

FILLING

- ½ pound spinach
- ¼ teaspoon salt
- 1½ cups whole-milk ricotta cheese
- 5 teaspoons grated parmesan cheese
- 1 egg
- Nutmeg
- Salt

TOPPING

- 2 ounces fontina cheese, finely diced (about ¼ cup)
- Freshly grated parmesan cheese

Make the pasta dough: Wash the spinach and remove the stems. Place in a nonaluminum saucepan and add the salt. Cover and cook over moderate heat for 12 to 15 minutes, until soft (if using frozen spinach, cook, covered, with salt, for 4 to 5 minutes). Let cool.

Squeeze the spinach dry; finely chop.

Pour the flour onto work surface. Shape into a mound and scoop a deep hollow in the center. Break the egg into the hollow; add the spinach. Mix the egg and spinach together with your fingers. Gradually mix in the flour, adding only enough to make a paste. The mixture should not be too dry.

Knead the dough on a lightly floured board, working in a bit more flour if dough seems sticky, until the dough is smooth, shiny, and elastic. Di-

vide the dough in half; using a pasta machine or a rolling pin, roll out the dough ¹⁄₁₆ inch thick.

Make the filling: Wash the spinach and remove stems. In a nonaluminum pan, combine the spinach with the salt. Cook, covered, for about 15 minutes, until tender. Squeeze dry; finely chop. In a bowl, mix the spinach with the ricotta, parmesan,

and egg. Season to taste with nutmeg and salt.

Place one sheet of pasta dough on a flat surface. Place 1 tablespoon dollops of the filling in rows about 2 inches apart, and about 1 inch from the top and sides. Place the other sheet of pasta lightly on top. Pat around the mounds lightly with your fingers. Using a pastry cutter, cut between the mounds, centering the filling in each square. Press down the edges.

Cook the tortelloni: In a large pot of slightly salted boiling water cook until just al dente, about 5 minutes.

A favorite way to end a meal in Aosta is with the *grolla*, a hand-carved wooden cup typical of the Valle d'Aosta. The *grolla*'s rim is lined with sugar, then lit; when the flame dies out, the cup is passed from guest to guest, and each takes a sip of the coffee and *grappa* mixture from one of the spigots. This communal drink is supposed to solidify the bonds of friendship.

Drain and place in an ovenproof baking dish. Sprinkle the fontina over the pasta. Place in a preheated 275°F. oven. Bake until cheese melts. Top with additional parmesan and serve.

Makes 4 to 6 servings

CAFFE ALLA VALDOSTANA

Valle d'Aosta Coffee

- **6 demitasse cups espresso coffee**
- **2 ounces *grappa***
- **2 tablespoons granulated sugar**
- **2 to 3 lemon or orange zests**

Combine the coffee, *grappa*, sugar, and lemon or orange zests in a *grolla*. The mixture should be piping hot. Remove the lid from the *grolla* and wet the rim with a bit of additional *grappa*. Sprinkle granulated sugar along the rim.

Caramelize the sugar by igniting it with a match. When the flames subside, spoon sugar into the coffee and cover with a lid.

Serves 5 to 6

MOUNTAIN HOUSES

Made of timber and stone, Italian mountain houses resemble Swiss chalets in many ways. The typical Italian Alpine dwelling has a broad gabled roof, long eaves supported by wood brackets, and facades trimmed with colorful shutters, hand-carved balconies, and wood grilles. Local farmers occupied these structures until the 1920s and 1930s, when the growing popularity of skiing attracted new people to the mountains. Original farmers' houses were suddenly in demand as vacation homes, particularly since many mountain towns prohibited new construction. These buildings were restored and modernized in considerable numbers after World War II.

The layout of remodeled mountain residences is traditional, with public rooms on the ground floor and bedrooms concentrated on the floor above. Interior style varies, becoming more fanciful and folkloric in the east, as one travels toward the Dolomites. But a certain eclectic clutter can be found in almost all Italian Alpine houses, where rooms are accented with collections of local crafts, such as antique pewter, copperware, glassware, and mugs, and wood and wax sculptures—along with dried flower arrangements.

The walls of most mountain houses are lined with boiserie, stone, or stucco, which is sometimes painted with naïf frescoes. Because paneled rooms filled with large wood pieces can be dark, fabrics for sofas, chairs, tablecloths, and curtains are generally white or vividly colored. Seventeenth- and 18th-century furniture embellished with *intaglio,* intricate relief work, are popular regional antiques.

Bedrooms in Italian Alpine houses can be extremely romantic. Beds with hand-carved headboards are draped in covers made from antique fabric, thick white lace, embroidered cottons, and piqués. Hand-painted wardrobes crafted in the South Tyrol and Alto Adige are decorated with natural and religious motifs. An essential element of both living rooms and bedrooms in the mountains is the *stufa,* or stove, covered in ceramic tile.

During the Christmas holidays, Italian Alpine houses are filled with white and red *stelle di Natale*—the Italians call poinsettias Christmas stars—baskets of pine boughs, and clusters of mistletoe. Bright red bows decorate stairways, doorway lintels, candelabra, and the Christmas tree. Lit with candles at night, and surrounded by glimmering snow, the Alpine chalet becomes a place of enchantment, warmth, and peace.

SMALL CHALET OVERLOOKING CORTINA

Rina Brion, the owner of Brionvega and known throughout Europe for bringing sleek Italian design to the styling of televisions, radios, and other electronic equipment, felt her mountain house should be anything but streamlined and modern. She never had enough room to display her favorite collections—among them Neapolitan crèche figurines, fans, and centuries-old ecclesiastical garments—until the small chalet overlooking Cortina she bought in the 1950s was restored and enlarged by architect Luigi Vietti.

The first level of the house is dominated by a large round living room completely rimmed with circular white sofas designed by Vietti. Red and white poinsettias fill windowsills and shelves behind the sofas during the holiday season. Although she likes to give parties, and her New Year's Day open house is an annual event in Cortina, most of the time she uses her mountain chalet as a quiet hideaway, where she can catch up on rest and reading.

Rina Brion indulged her taste for the romantic when furnishing the master bedroom and guest rooms. All bed coverings and many of the curtains are white, trimmed with ruffles and embroidery. "Cortina is such a fantasy land when it's covered with snow," says the industrialist. "I wanted to create the same atmosphere in the rooms upstairs which have windows that look out on the mountains and town. It was an attempt to capture some of the magic of the place."

Although crafted in recent times, the door, left, leading to the Brion house has a diamond pattern, which is a traditional motif in the Dolomites. The small windows covered with iron grates are also typical of mountain houses. Long eaves, right, protect the entrance and balconies from heavy snowfalls.

Antique bisque angels frame the wood-relief Nativity scene crafted in Holland in the 1400s, above. The crèche, left, placed on a living room table is from Tuscany. In the 18th century, the figurines of Italian Nativity scenes were often dressed in rich clothing. Mountain wildflowers, dried and arranged in small bouquets, are frequently found in Italian Alpine houses, right.

Italian pewter and majolica trim a shelf of the walnut Tuscan *armadio,* which dates from Renaissance times, right. The small armless chair is from the Ampezzo region of the Dolomites.

The Genoan fourposter, left, in the guest bedroom, is typical of Italian beds made during the 16th and 17th centuries. Head- and baseboards were often replaced with posts embellished with turnery and gilding. The bed linens and hand-embroidered piqué pillowcases, right, are Venetian with the exception of the big cushion, which was hand-made in the Marches region.

A Venetian lace antimacassar serves as a runner on the bedroom's large Ampezzano chest. The silver hand mirror is also Venetian.

The Marzotto family added wings to both sides of their Cortina farmhouse, top. The open balcony on the second floor and the enclosed terrace on the third are ideal for morning and afternoon sunbathing. Marta Marzotto's red velvet cushions cover even outdoor benches during the Christmas holidays, above.

HOME FOR CHRISTMAS

The Marzotto family, when describing their Cortina home, will say *"É molto vissuto"*—it's very lived in. A rambling three-level dwelling, it is one of the liveliest places in Cortina. The Marzottos' sons and daughters always seem to be leaving or returning from the slopes, friends stop by at all hours of the day, grandchildren roam through the rooms, and the Marzottos are usually on their way to or hosting a luncheon or dinner party. Their New Year's Eve *festa,* attended by over two hundred people, is *the* event of Cortina's holiday social season.

All rooms are abundant in detail. Antiques and regional artifacts— pewter, collections of *argenti poveri,* the "poor silver," which is Venetian glass painted with a mirrored surface, and rare figurines made of wax called *ceri* reflect the richness of popular crafts in the Ampezzo and South Tyrol. Painted wardrobes from the 19th century are used throughout the house, the most beautiful one of all located in the living room.

In some ways it is the ultimate Christmas house. The public rooms on the ground floor are decorated in red and green, red chosen by the family "because it's a happy color" and green "because it's so peaceful." The color scheme is accented by red cyclamen, red poinsettias, and white orchids during the holidays.

"The decor is very much in keeping with the Marzottos' spirited approach to life," comments a friend, architect Luigi Vietti. But it's also ideally suited to a mountain home in these parts, where things have traditionally been quite colorful and folkloric."

A metal cover serves as a baffle to prevent cold air from entering the chimney, right, and forces smoke back into the room. The baffle is also a graphic accent on the roof.

Marta Marzotto, above, is one of Cortina's most active hostesses and a skier who dresses with noted color and style. A small sled, left, used by the Marzottos' grandchildren, lies abandoned near the woods surrounding the chalet.

The living room's large red sofa, above, is decorated with pillows designed by Marta Marzotto, and the whimsical checker game, with markers of red and green apples. The wardrobe, below, was painted in the *arte povera* style by South Tyrolean farmers at the beginning of the 19th century.

An oversized *panettone* on the kitchen table, left, awaits a hungry crowd of family members and friends at the end of a day's skiing. The kitchen door was hand-painted with Tyrolean motifs by local artisans.

CONDOMINIUM WITH ALPINE ANTIQUES

The Amorusos, a Roman couple who love to ski, were tired of staying in hotels during winter holidays. They decided to look for a *pied-à-terre* that required little upkeep in a mountain town that had some nightlife, and friends suggested Cortina. When they quickly found a small apartment near the village, they considered themselves lucky indeed.

Although a contemporary condominium in Cortina can be as colorless as its equivalent in an urban high-rise, the Amorusos decided to buy the place rather than lose the prized location and were determined to "age" it by giving each room some Ampezzano flavor. The couple scouted the area for antique paneling, beams, and split logs that date from the 17th, 18th, and 19th centuries. A local carpenter covered the walls of the apartment with carefully fitted pieces of old wood and installed a beautiful hand-painted coffered ceiling that Liliana Amoruso found in a Veneto villa. Once the apartment's new "old" interior shell was finished, the owners bought 17th- and 18th-century furniture from the Ampezzo and South Tyrol and a collection of rare naïf paintings depicting mountain scenes.

A large balcony provides mountain views and, when the sun shines, a place for sunbathing. "It's not unusual for us to have lunch outdoors in the winter," says Liliana Amoruso, "and in February the balcony is so warm that I lie here in my bikini."

The apartment is small, but it includes a guest room, and the Amorusos also own a studio apartment on the ground floor of the building, which serves as a guest suite. When in Cortina, the couple and their friends use the apartments as a base, but everyone is usually out skiing or attending parties.

Decorative toy squirrels enliven a latticed screen on the terrace, top. The terrace faces south and affords views of woods filled with pines and a horizon bordered by the Dolomites, above. Liliana Amoruso, left, a resident of Rome, often dresses in native Ampezzano costume when entertaining guests in her apartment.

The large building, left, modeled after a chalet, is one of a few in Cortina that contain a dozen or so condominiums.

A 17th-century hand-painted coffered ceiling, above, and 18th-century paneling, right, were installed in the contemporary apartment to give it an antique flavor. The horseman, dressed in glittering clothes, below, was crafted in the South Tyrol in the 18th century and now hangs on a living-room wall.

For the small eat-in kitchen, right, the Amorusos lined walls with contemporary paneling. The pretzel-shaped breads reflect the Austrian influence in Ampezzano cuisine.

A small guest room, right, can sleep two. The little table was made from an old hatbox and the chair is a mid-18th-century regional piece.

RESTORED HAYLOFT

Architect Luigi Vietti bought an 18th-century *toulà*, or hayloft, in 1942 as a mountain getaway for himself and his bride, Riccarda. He began the restoration of the modest farmhouse during the war, having to abandon it when the Germans occupied Cortina. Luckily for Vietti, the house wasn't destroyed—the town was declared a hospital zone and escaped bombardment.

A great admirer of regional architecture, Vietti sought to modify the original structure as little as possible, while making it comfortable for two- and three-week winter stays and informal entertaining. Constructed in 1752, the

Once a farmer's hayloft, Vietti's *toulà*, below and right, is Cortina's oldest privately owned dwelling. The first two floors are made of stone, the third, where the hay used to be stored, entirely of wood.

building is Cortina's oldest farmhouse still occupied by a single family, and thanks to the architect's meticulous, historically attentive restoration, it is also the archetypal *toulà* in Cortina today.

Vietti left the wood and stone facade untouched, but installed several large windows in the back of the structure to allow more light to enter the living area. He kept what was once the upper hayloft open, and used furniture to organize the space into various zones for dining, conversation, and watching television. An open hearth in one corner of the living room provides an additional conversation spot and cooking area, too. Vietti then restored the original log flooring and modernized the bathrooms, but covered their walls with traditional split beams and stucco.

Architect Luigi Vietti, below, was responsible for restoring many of Cortina's farmhouses and is one of Italy's best-known architects. Curtains trim all the *toulà*'s windows, right.

The *toulà*'s original bedrooms became the master bedroom and guest rooms. Each has a large, high bed crafted in the region. "Beds were made to be as much as four feet off the ground in the Ampezzo," says Vietti. "Since heat rises, a tall bed stayed warmer longer than one close to the floor." The rooms are heated by built-in *stufe* near the beds.

Vietti converted the attic into a studio for himself, and an additional guest bedroom, adding several small windows that look out on Cortina's famous mountain peaks, the Tofana and the Folaria. The studio has been used extensively over the past four decades, as after his work on his own home, Vietti became the most highly esteemed and sought-after architect in Cortina.

The former hayloft was sectioned into various sitting areas, above left. The staircase dates from the *toulà*'s construction. The dining room table, left, was made from an antique wood plank that was 3½ meters.

The Vietti house is filled with guests and family during Christmas. Even in a town where there's a party every night, the Viettis' gatherings are extremely popular. Champagne and sparkling wine flows, the cuisine is local Ampezzano and South Tyrolean, and the desserts are so tempting that even the slimmest and most chic of Italian *principesse* become amnesic about their diets. The Viettis hold a large dinner party on the night of the Epiphany, officially the last event of the holiday season in Cortina. They stay on until mid-January, return in February for the wildly festive *Carnevale,* and then close the house for the year.

Red velvet pillows, left, hand-embroidered with flowers by Sardinian craftswomen, are arranged on the living-room sofa. Glass mugs, above left, are from the Ampezzo and South Tyrol.

123

Walls of the master bathroom, below, were covered with old logs.

A decorative *stufa*, above, can be found in most Ampezzano homes. This one was made in Genoa during the 1500s.

The bed in the master bedroom, left, has a baldachin of white Lombardy lace and cotton piqué. A Nativity scene, arranged in a niche in the bedroom, was sculpted by Venetian artisans.

DOCTOR'S FAMILY HOUSE NEAR MONT BLANC

Being a doctor in a ski town means receiving plenty of emergency calls during the winter season, so when Dr. Giuseppe Forremento and his wife, Yole, were planning to build a new family house, one of their primary requirements was that it be located near the main Valle d'Aosta road linking Courmayeur and its medical facilities with other nearby villages. The Forrementos were lucky to find property close to this thoroughfare—not only was it ideally situated, but it also allowed outstanding views of Mont Blanc. In the mid-1970s, they constructed a chalet on the

The stone window with wrought-iron grille was found in a Valdostano castle and installed in the wall between the living and dining rooms, left. The Forrementos are year-round residents of the stone and stucco chalet, below, near Courmayeur.

grounds and designed an enormous window in the dining area to take advantage of the impressive panorama.

A great-grandson of the main architect to the Italian Royal House of Savoy, Dr. Forremento inherited his family's interest in furniture and their passion for collecting. Whenever his schedule permitted, he attended local auctions in small Valdostano villages, looking for pieces crafted in the region. From houses about to be demolished, he purchased doors, window casements, and banisters, as well as furniture. Most of the furnishings Dr. Forremento bought for the chalet date from the 1600s, and they range from farmer's stools used for milking cows to hand-carved chestnut wardrobes that were found in crumbling castles. Some of his favorite finds include antique toys, pewter mugs, and old books filled with etchings of local scenes.

As full-time residents of Courmayeur, the Forrementos are able to enjoy the quiet beauty of the mountains during the week, when most of the skiers have returned to Turin and Milan. Undaunted by snowstorms that occur daily at certain times of the year, strong winds blowing off the mountains, and dense fog, the doctor makes his rounds, helping his neighbors to get well and skiers to get back on the slopes, keeping his eyes open now and then for an unusual antique—or another piece of pewter.

The hand-carved 17th-century Valdostano chest, left, is topped with the Forrementos' collection of pewter plates and pitchers crafted in the Valle d'Aosta in the 17th, 18th, and 19th centuries. Pieces from the pewter collection also frame the dining area, below. The 17th-century dining table, like all the antique furniture in the house, received a protective coat of wax to help preserve and beautify its old wood.

White and brown ceramic tiles harmonize with the white walls and deep brown tones of the 18th-century Piedmontese table and doors in the eat-in kitchen. Like many people who live informally in the mountains, the Forrementos prefer the kitchen to the dining room for their midday meal.

VILLA WITH CHAPELS AND CLOISTERS

Commanding a sweeping view of Courmayeur, the large villa is one of the most striking residences in the region. Constructed by a Milanese architect for Count Tondani in the 1930s, it is now the summer and holiday retreat of the Natale family, who also have homes in Milan and the Veneto. Villa Tondani, as the house is still called, blends well with other older structures in the Poussey residential district, which is within walking distance of the village. Because the original owners were quite religious, there's a chapel on the property, connected to the main house by graceful cloisters.

Cloisters and a chapel abut the Tondani villa in the Poussey residential district of Courmayeur, above left. Finished with school by midday, two young Italians enjoy the latest snowfall, left.

Fanciful wrought-iron gates surround the house and cloisters, above. The stone villa, left, built by the late Count Tondani in the 1930s, is considered one of the most beautiful in town. Religious frescoes, decorative stone balconies, and intricately carved doors enrich the facade.

While the furnishings are primarily useful and sturdy Valdostano pieces from the early 1900s, the architectural detailing is elaborate. Local craftsmen sculpted wood and marble banisters in a variety of Valdostano patterns for balconies, carved snowflake designs in the wood shutters, stenciled nature motifs into the windows, and created decorative wrought-iron grilles for the entrance of the cloisters and property. The kitchen ceiling, the coffered bedroom ceilings, and the bedroom and bathroom walls have been covered with frescoes.

Villa Tondani has three floors and more than a dozen rooms. To make the house more manageable, the Natale family converted the second and third levels into apartments that are rented out year-round. During the winter, when frequent snowfalls powder the house, cloisters, chapel, trees, and shrubs, the property is at its most beautiful—the ideal spot for an unhurried and very peaceful stay, according to Adriana Natale.

In most Valle d'Aosta houses, mantelpieces are made of wood, but the stone mantel, with its intricately carved frieze, probably came from a local castle or *palazzo*. The soft light from the fireplace makes the ochre stucco walls seem golden.

Frescoes decorate the kitchen ceiling, above, and the small arched niche in the bathroom, below right. They were painted by local artisans at the time of the villa's construction.

Wood and copper kitchen utensils made in the Valle d'Aosta fill the walls of the simple country kitchen, left. Cupboards and cabinets were also crafted in the area.

PART III

THE LAKE COUNTRY IN SPRING

Lake Como and Lake Maggiore

The Lombardy lakes, Como and Maggiore, delight the visitor with a landscape and climate that is part Alpine and part Mediterranean. Here one sees snow-capped mountains in the distance and palm trees along the shore, pine forests and gardens filled with jasmine, camellias, and oleander. Early in the day, mountain breezes cool the lakes with fresh Alpine air. Breezes with a balmy

tropical feel relieve the heat of the late afternoon. Some lakeside towns have a pristine Swiss appearance, while others have the *dolce vita* allure of the Riviera. • There's a touch of Venice, too, in and around the lakes. Lichen-covered landing docks and baroque wrought-iron gates mark the entrances to lakeside villas and hotels. Lacquered teak motorboats, sleek hydrofoils, and small tourist and commuter steamers churn up waters on the lakes as steadily as the traffic does on the Grand Canal. Instead of Venetian gondolas, local fishing boats topped with hoop-shaped iron frames are reminders of the past. • In the 18th and 19th centuries, Europe's *belle gente* visited the Lombard lake district, and it remains one of Italy's most elegant areas. The palm tree-lined promenades of resort towns with their grand old hotels, stately villas, and enormous gardens, still suggest grandeur and

ease. ● The lakes were popular until World War II. In the 1950s and 1960s, the Mediterranean seaside became a favorite spring and summer vacation spot for Italians and lured many people from the lakes. But Como and Maggiore have enjoyed a renaissance in the last decade. The Milanese have come back to the lakes, whether to buy and restore a lakeside villa, or to relax a few days in a lovely, quiet hotel on the water. The lakes' proximity to Milan, an abundance of boating and water sports facilities, new country clubs, and uncrowded beaches have all contributed to the revival. ● The lake area is a treat to the senses. In the morning you wake to hear water softly lapping the shores and *campanili* bells chiming the hours from tiny towns kilometers away. In the afternoon you can enjoy picnics in fragrant lakeside gardens, a swim in the cooling waters, a visit to a historic villa, or a tour of the lake on a slow-moving ferryboat. A favorite way to end a day of such pleasures is to have dinner on a high hill overlooking the night-blackened water with its rhinestone trim of towns.

LAKE VIEWS

Lombardy's loveliest lake? Without a doubt it's **Lake Como,** say many Italians. Writers through the ages have backed up this claim. Virgil considered the lake area one of the great splendors of the peninsula and centuries later Longfellow wrote, "Is there a land of such supreme and perfect beauty anywhere?"

Como's lakeside towns were first settled during the Roman Republic, but the lake's gilded era began in the mid-1700s and lasted until the days of the Belle Epoque. The Romantics—writers, opera composers, and painters—immortalized Como's charms, inspiring a host of titled Europeans to visit. Italian, French, Austrian, German, and English nobles put Como on the social map by building great villas along its shores and inviting a steady steam of prominent friends for long holidays. Napoleon attended the opening of the Villa Olmo, then home to the Odescalchi, a leading Roman family. A princess of Wales, Caroline of Brunswick, later the estranged queen of King George IV, took up residence in what is now the Villa d'Este, purportedly to be able to carry out

With its elaborate gardens, grand country villas, and gracious way of life, the Italian lake district is one of Italy's most enchanting regions, left. As in other sections of the Italian countryside, the roofs of buildings are covered with terra-cotta tiles, right. A serene formal garden, overleaf, is on an island in Lake Maggiore.

her numerous assignations far from foggy London. A Russian empress lived at the villa, too, but with much less fanfare. In recent times, government leaders like Winston Churchill and Konrad Adenauer came to Como to relax.

The western branch of the wishbone-shaped lake, from the towns of Como to Menaggio, is the prettiest part of a very pretty area. This stretch of lake and countryside is worth viewing by boat and by car. From the water, you see villas peeking out behind curtains of evergreens, stone houses linked together by old, arched bridges, and Italians lounging at lakeside pools in pursuit of tans that are as golden as their Bulgari jewelry. Every time a steamer goes by, boats in the harbors of fishing villages rock like bathtub toys, and the lake, which looks pudding thick when still, becomes covered with a wake of foamy waves.

One narrow road connects all the lakeside villages. A stalled auto, a lazy goat, or a stoplight gone amiss will create traffic jams that back up cars all the way from Como to Menaggio. But blocked traffic often turns into a grand

roadside party. Rather than honking their horns, drivers as well as passengers are fond of abandoning their cars for a few moments to enjoy the view or eat some bread, cheese, and fruit al fresco.

The part of the lake shore that runs from Lenno to Tremezzo is often referred to as the Azalea Riviera. Most lakeside gardens have more than their fair share of the colorful plant, but it seems to thrive particularly well in this less hilly area, which is full of sun. The garden of the Villa Carlotta in Tremezzo has long walkways lined with six-foot-high rows of azaleas and rhododendrons that are trimmed and used as hedges.

Opposite Tremezzo, accessible by boat from Cadenabbia, is the resort town of Bellagio. It stands on the promontory that divides the parts of the wishbone in two. A medieval town tightly packed with narrow streets, Bellagio has imposing residences outside its center with some of the most alluring gardens you'll find anywhere along the lake. For example, those of the Villa Melzi and Villa Serbelloni seem like paradise. The Grand Hotel Villa Serbelloni in Bellagio and the Villa d'Este across the water in Cernobbio have great style, and with the exception of owning a lakeside villa, the two luxury hotels are the best places to experience the elegant country life that was once the exclusive entitlement of Europe's best-known aristocrats.

Because of the lack of flat terrain surrounding Lake Como, villages and churches hug the shore and many houses are built on steep hills and mountain slopes. Narrow roads connect the uppermost reaches of the mountains with the city of Como.

Large and luminous **Lake Maggiore** is claimed by the regions of Lombardy and Piedmont, as well as by Switzerland. Silvery waters reflect villas, tropical gardens, and even the profile of an entire town. Many parts of the lake and its surrounding landscape can be so tranquil that the only movement comes from clouds drifting slowly through the sky.

Maggiore's 40-mile shoreline reveals a variety of scenery that attracted such diverse guests in the 19th century as Queen Victoria and Thomas Mann. Fishing villages with weather-worn town houses and narrow cobblestoned streets are tucked between resorts

like Stresa and Baveno with huge Belle Epoque hotels, where it is easy to imagine a turn-of-the-century parade of grande dames swirling parasols as they strolled along the flower-lined quays. Stucco *palazzi* and shrub- and tree-covered mountains in the southern part of the lake give way to little wooden houses with red shutters and sloping roofs, and snow-draped Alps as you travel into Switzerland.

Seven islands dot the lake; the most beautiful belong to the Borromeo archipelago. Two of the Borromean islands, Isola Bella and Isola Madre, are lavish souvenirs of the baroque era, while tiny Isola dei Pescatori seems like an island time capsule—life has changed little over the centuries for its several hundred inhabitants who earn their living as fishermen. On Maggiore's eastern shore a 14th-century Gothic castle, once home to the Viscontis and owned for hundreds of years by the Borromeo family, stands on a mighty base, the Rocca d'Angera, which plunges dramatically into the water. With its breathtaking views of the lake's central basin, the fortress-castle

allows the visitor to see how an aristocratic family lived on Lake Maggiore during the Middle Ages.

To enjoy Maggiore to the fullest, you should tour it by boat. Each day steamers depart from Arona at the southern tip of the lake and stop at all the major towns before ending the run in Locarno, Switzerland, about four hours later. Lakeside towns near Switzerland have a mild climate year-round—camellias bloom even in the winter—and are popular resorts during the winter as well as the spring and summer.

A visit to a small lakeside town on its market day will afford pleasures of another kind. The market in Luino, held each

Wednesday, is known for its clothing, food, ceramics, and housewares, and attracts visitors from Milan and Turin, as well as Swiss buyers, who fill the little village with Mercedes and Rolls-Royces. If you're thinking of a casual picnic, you can purchase all you need at the market—fresh local breads and cheese, wine, slices of prosciutto, grapes, blood oranges, raspberries, and blackberries. Or you may prefer to stop by a simple trattoria. While the sole waiter, usually the son, brother, or nephew of the owner, may recite the daily offerings in the place of a printed menu, and then go out to the garden to pick salad greens, your meal can be extremely memorable, and rival the cooking of better-known restaurants along the lake.

During the week, the waters of Lake Como are tranquil. On weekends, the lake is crisscrossed by pleasure craft, hydrofoils, and ferries, which stop at towns along the shore, right.

Small fishing boats with hoop frames are characteristic of the northern lakes, above left. The rounded frames are covered with canvas when the weather is bad and when the boats are pulled ashore after fishing. The Borromeo Palace, right, dominates the tiny island of Isola Bella in the middle of Lake Maggiore.

LOCAL COLORS

Deep velvetlike blue greens and a range of terra-cotta tones give Lake Como a romantic coloring. On sunny days the lake looks ever-green, and the pine, oak, and chestnut trees on the mountains and hills that tightly enclose the lake take on a rich blue cast. To contrast with the sweep of greens and blues, *comaschi,* the people who live in and near Como, like to paint their buildings in warm pink, salmon, rose, and sienna hues. Blue-green gardens turn almost completely red or violet in the spring, when rhododendrons and azaleas bloom.

Lake Maggiore's more open landscape is a spectrum of blues. The water seems sapphire. The mountains, often covered by a gauze-like haze, appear slate blue, even navy blue when viewed from a distance. Garlands of thick white clouds lazily roll over mountaintops and trim the bottom of the unusually bright blue sky.

Large terra-cotta urns planted with pink geraniums, top, are common elements in lakeside gardens. A cluster of rich green lily pads, far left, shelters a duck in a lakeside garden pond. During the 19th century, many villas had frescoed facades, but today most exteriors are monochromatic. The terra-cotta color of a villa in Campo, left, on the western shore of Lake Como, is in vivid contrast to the green cypresses that surround it.

The new wing of the Villa d'Este Hotel has a trompe l'oeil facade and Gothic and Renaissance details in terra-cotta and ochre hues, above. For a luncheon by Lake Como, the rose- and deep-blue-toned table linens, right, were chosen to match the colors of the lakeside landscape. At night, the lakes often appear a rich blue, far right, and the lights of villages sparkle along the distant shoreline.

WATER SPORTS

The northern Italian lakes provide glorious settings for water sports. Mountain breezes make the lakes ideal for windsurfing and sailing. Regatta races are held on holidays during the spring and summer, and, viewed from the mountain roads, the dozens of small sailboats look like white rose petals drifting across the water.

Bathers appear at lakeside beaches and country clubs mid-morning, and, with an attitude of *dolce far niente* (it's nice to do nothing), take leisurely dips in the lake or in the country club pool, then proceed to work on their tans. But waterskiers race through the placid lake waters like training jets darting through the sky. Drivers of the often flashy speedboats exhibit the same daring and quick reflexes you see daily on most Italian roads.

The lakes can become quite crowded on summer weekends. But traveling north on both Como and Maggiore, the traffic thins out. You can sail for kilometers in solitude, with only the occasional local fisherman in his tiny rowboat as a companion on the water.

Devotees of water skiing, left, and sunbathing, inset left, can enjoy their pastime in spring because of the lake region's mild climate. The Villa d'Este built its pool, right, out into the lake, providing visitors with two options for swimming. Lakeside restaurants offer light midday snacks in spring and summer, inset right.

THE SILKS OF COMO

For the finishing and printing of luxury silks, Como is now the unrivaled world capital. Since World War II, Como fabric manufacturers have stolen the limelight from the French who, from their mills in Lyon, dominated the quality silk market in Europe for years. Italian designers have always considered themselves lucky to have their fabric sources so close at hand, and today, even top French couturiers come to Como, along with noted American and English designers.

One of the reasons Milan developed into a fashion center was, in fact, its proximity to Como. Italian fabric know-how was an integral factor in the success of the country's ready-to-wear designers in the 1970s. Newcomers like Armani, Versace, and Ferrè worked closely with Como manufacturers, who were willing to interpret just about any idea or whim into beautiful fabric, as well as to back the new designers financially. In the competitive world of couture and *prêt-à-porter* fashion, the Italian designers' fabric allies gave them a much-needed edge against the French.

Most textile companies in Como have been owned and operated by a single family for decades. Though mindful of tradition, Como silk producers pride themselves on their innovative colors and blends, and the consistent quality of their fabrics. They will boast of machines that produce 50 shades of a single color, tell you about their new gossamer blends of silk and wool, or even a waterproof silk. They will proudly admit that 8 percent of their profits is devoted to research, and how it is a love for their work and the desire to keep producing better silk and more sophisticated prints that keep them motivated to be leaders in their field. Firmly established as fashion suppliers, many silk companies have turned their sights to the production of fine fabrics for home furnishings, and their entry into this new market has been widely applauded by interior designers throughout the world.

At the Mantero silk-finishing factory near Como, newly printed scarves are laid out to dry, far left. Antique hand-carved pear tree wood blocks, left, with classic decorative patterns, are on display in the factory. The colors, right, used in silk printing are made from both natural and chemical dyes.

WROUGHT IRON

The Spaniards, who dominated Lombardy in the 1500s, may have introduced wrought iron to the region. But it was most likely the local aristocrats and the architects of their villas along the lakes in the 17th and 18th centuries who created the taste for ornate wrought iron. Influenced by the baroque style sweeping the peninsula, the nobles wanted even the most functional elements in their villas, like protective gates and grilles, to be extremely ornamental. The taste for elaborate wrought-iron treatments for gates, window coverings, balconies, and terraces survived into

An elaborate gate crafted in the mid-18th century, left, greets visitors who arrive by boat at a lakeside villa. The wrought-iron garden chair, below, was inspired by a Louis XV fauteuil, and on the first warm, clear day of spring is still missing its cushion.

the 19th century when even more grand houses were built in the lake area, and it continues to the present.

Approaching a lakeside villa either by water or by land, the first thing you see is a large wrought-iron gate, sometimes as fanciful as the formal gardens it protects. Wrought-iron elements are used indoors as well in lakeside houses. Banisters, candelabra, lighting fixtures, even coat racks are crafted from metal—and pieces from earlier periods are highly valued for their workmanship and design.

In a private garden of a baroque *palazzo*, a princely Italian family opted for simple wrought-iron lawn furniture painted a vivid yellow, left. A small stone-topped garden table with elaborately curved wrought-iron feet, below, adds a fanciful touch in a quiet corner of a lakeside garden. The decorative banister, right, in architect Giacomo Mantegazza's house, dates from the 1920s.

LIGHT MEALS BY THE LAKE

While the lake area is unique within Lombardy and Italy, the food served in restaurants and villas along Lakes Maggiore and Como is similar to what you might find in Milan. The staples of Lombard cuisine include rice, veal, fowl, and rich soft cheeses like Gorgonzola, mascarpone, and stracchino.

Favorite first courses in Lombardy are rice dishes such as *risotto alla Milanese,* prepared with saffron, and *minestrone alla Milanese,* a thick vegetable soup which is served hot in the winter and cold in the summer. *Ossobuco,* a stew made with a braised veal shank, and *costolette Milanese,* thin scaloppine dipped in bread crumbs and lightly sautéed, are classic entrees. Lombardy has given Italy

Most midday *pranzi* at lakeside villas during the spring and summer tend to be light buffets enjoyed al fresco, left.

two of its best-known sweet breads, *panettone*, which looks like a chef's hat and is studded with raisins and candied fruits, and *colomba*, shaped like a dove and sprinkled with crystallized sugar and almonds. Although it is now eaten year-round, *panettone* is the traditional Christmas cake in northern Italy, while *colomba* is usually found in bakeries around Easter.

In Lombardy, considered Italy's most modern region, businesses don't usually close for the customary two-hour break, and lunch is often a light meal—sometimes just a plate of mozzarella, fresh tomatoes, and basil, or prosciutto and melon or figs. During the late spring and summer many Italian men and women, ever conscious of the lean figure they should be cutting at poolside or on the decks of their boats, opt for these simple low-calorie dishes.

With an abundance of fresh fruit, cheese, and delicious cured meats, a tasty luncheon can be prepared in a few moments. *Carpaccio* topped with thin slivers of *parmigiano*, left, and the classic combination of mozzarella, tomatoes, and basil, right, are favorite dishes in the spring and summer. An elegant *macedonia di frutta*, above, makes a perfect springtime dessert.

LAKESIDE HOUSES AND GARDENS

 Most lakeside houses in Como and Maggiore were built during the 18th and 19th centuries by aristocrats and industrialists who could afford to have a second home. Privileged families would often leave their urban *palazzi* for lakeside holidays in late spring and return to town only in autumn. They wanted their villas to be suitable for these luxurious sojourns and lavish entertaining, and frequently modeled them after Florentine *palazzi*, although on a much larger scale. Villas included at least three levels. A ground floor had numerous large reception rooms and smaller sitting rooms. Grand-scale salons with marble floors and columns were ideal settings for big dinner parties, balls, and concerts. On the floor above, the *piano nobile* contained the most important bedrooms and guest rooms. The third level consisted of mezzanines and the attic, where the domestic staff of visiting houseguests had their tiny rooms. In an era when guests would come for months at a time, ample space for servants was essential.

Villas were decorated in the elegant fashion of the day—with neoclassical, Empire, Napoleon III, or Venetian baroque pieces. Although life on the lake is far more relaxed than it was one hundred years ago, many houses are still furnished with these period antiques. The 19th century's gentleman of means would probably find himself quite at home.

Formal Italian gardens surround most villas. Tall hedges of azaleas, seas of rhododendron, acres of flower beds, lily ponds bordered by stone cherubs, balustraded terraces, box trees and yews trimmed in fancy patterns are some of the elements of lakeside gardens that have been admired and copied throughout the world. The landscape gardening is extraordinary at many of the largest estates, some of which have been turned into hotels, while others have been designated historical landmarks and are now open for public viewing. The grounds of the most imposing villas might also have parks filled with tropical plants and flowers. Smaller villas that are still privately owned incorporate some of the garden design of the great estates, although in a less imposing way.

ARCHITECT'S PRIVATE RETREAT

The only way to get to architect Giacomo Mantegazza's exquisite weekend and summer villa in the tiny Lake Como hamlet of Campo is by boat. Mr. Mantegazza picks up most of his guests in Campo or Lenno, small towns located along mid-lake shores, and transports them in the kind of hoop-framed boat that has been used in the region for centuries to his lakeside house, La Cassinella. The rambling 19th-century villa was restored in the 1920s by Mantegazza's father, who considered it "the loveliest villa he ever worked on." The Mantegazzas have been Como architects for four generations.

When the villa's elderly American owner decided she was no longer fit for transatlantic travel, she put the house on the market and Mantegazza rushed to buy it. Consisting of the villa, guest house, gardener's house, tennis court, and spacious gardens, the compound was ideal for the architect's large and lively family— he has eight children.

Used infrequently in the decade prior to its sale in 1974, the house was nonetheless in excellent condition. Mantegazza kept the exterior color his father had chosen—a rich salmon, brightened with blue shutters. He furnished the villa with central and northern Italian rustic antiques from the 17th, 18th, and 19th centuries in a style that was "gracious, yet realistic for a large family." After the interior was

The villa has a facade trimmed with ivy and a landing dock bordered by stately cypresses, left. The shutters were painted blue to harmonize with the color of the lake. Statues of *putti*, cherubs, are frequently found in lakeside garden lily ponds, right.

165

The entrance hall, right, was painted a light ochre to blend with the marble floor. The 16th-century table, which once was used in a library, is Tuscan. In the dining room, below right, Giacomo Mantegazza created a rustic chandelier, actually three wrought-iron candelabra mounted upside down, to complement the late Renaissance country furniture.

completed, Mantegazza revitalized the informal English-style garden on the sloping terrain behind the villa.

Located in one of the most secluded parts of Lake Como, La Cassinella is never completely tranquil on weekends during the summer. The Mantegazza children arrive by boat with friends, windsurf and waterski on the lake, and squeeze in a few rounds of tennis. Giacomo Mantegazza, his wife, Stefania, and youngest son, David, are the only ones who ever seem to sit down beneath the entrance portico for *pranzo*, and a few moments of relaxation.

The origin of the clothes rack, right, is unknown, but this is an unusual piece, even in a region where many decorative elements are made from wrought iron.

The master bedroom, left, is graciously furnished with 17th- and 18th-century antiques from northern and central Italy, which Giacomo Mantegazza has collected over the years. The doors, above, with hand-painted panels, are from the Marches, a region in the center of Italy near the Adriatic. The 17th-century Italian desk has legs carved *a rocchetto*, in spoollike shapes, a detail frequently found in Italian Renaissance and baroque furniture.

169

As he visited antiques fairs and shops throughout Italy, Giacomo Mantegazza continually added to his collection of antique artifacts. The table, left, probably made for a farmer's home around 1650, holds an old bottle opener, bolt, fruit press bowl, and keys. Nail studs were popular decorative elements in the Renaissance, as evident from the 15th-century door and armchair, right.

The Mantegazzas decided to
cover a good deal of their hilly
property with lawn, above, rather
than attempt a formal lakeside
garden, which is more suited to
an expanse of flat land. As the
villa is accessible only by water,
Giacomo Mantegazza, right, must
commute to a nearby dock to
pick up houseguests.

Terra-cotta tiles, above, provide good insulation and their rounded shape allows rainwater to drain off easily. A stone mask, left, accents a wall of the villa. Doric columns, right, line a loggia at the back of the villa.

EARLY RENAISSANCE PALAZZO BY THE LAKE

Michele Canepa, a member of a well-known *comasca* family involved in silk manufacturing for over a century, grew up in a villa on the shores of Lake Como. "I have extremely fond memories of the lake," says Mr. Canepa, head of the family textile concern. "And when I married I thought I should have an environment similar to one I knew as a child for my own children to enjoy."

In 1980 he and his wife, the German-born fashion designer Harriet Selling, began to search both banks of the western branch of Lake Como for a weekend and summer house. "Many of the oldest and prettiest villas were too large or too difficult to get to," recalls Harriet Canepa, who spent close to a year looking for an appropriate place. Through German friends she heard that one of the lake's oldest villas, the 15th-century Villa Balbiano, was up for sale. "We considered it quite a find. Not too many *comaschi,* including my husband,

were familiar with it, as it had been owned by foreigners for decades. It's one of the most beautiful villas on the lake, and one of the few that dates from the early Renaissance."

Proportioned like a Florentine *palazzo,* the villa has a variety of classical details that were added over the centuries. Walls are covered with delicately colored 18th-century frescoes depicting Roman scenes. Intricate stuccowork, adorned with eagles and other Empire-inspired touches, trim ceilings in the salons and halls.

Villa Balbiano, left, now owned by the Canepa family, is one of Lake Como's few remaining Renaissance villas. The building's symmetrical design allows glimpses of the lake from the front lawn, above.

"The villa remains somewhat underfurnished," explains Harriet Canepa. "Originally it was because my husband and I had little time to search for antiques. But we came to like the way many of the frescoed rooms looked without much in them." The large salons on the first and second floors are practically empty, which is just fine with their young son, Max, who likes to tear through them on his tricycle or with the huge family Doberman, Hannibal. The salons are also a comfortable setting for the large parties the Canepas throw during the summer, which are attended by a young and fashionable Milanese crowd.

A formal garden dominates the entrance to the villa. Cardinal Durini, a resident of Villa Balbiano in the 1700s, designed it to

In the spring and summer, a small pergola overlooking the garden and the lake, left, serves as an outdoor dining room. Max Canepa, below, likes the garden's long paths, where he can drive his tricycle.

Because the Alps protect the lake region from northern winds and storms, the area has a mild climate that allows such tropical vegetation as palm trees, above, to thrive.

Comasco native Michele Canepa, head of Giovanni Canepa, a well-known Como textile firm, and his wife, fashion designer Harriet Selling, visit their lakeside house with their son, Max, left, throughout the year.

Harriet Selling Canepa purchased the Raquel Welch figure, whose creator is unknown, at an art show in Paris. An 18th-century Venetian divan can be seen through the doorway of a second-level bedroom.

resemble those found in Tuscany during the Renaissance. "Although the garden is still large, it was once a kilometer in length and reached to the foot of the nearest mountain!" says Michele Canepa. "Most lakeside gardens have to be built on slopes, because of the hilly terrain in the area, but this one is unusual for Como because it is long and flat." The grounds that border the lake at the back of the villa contain a casual assortment of pine, cypress, palm, and citrus

trees, and a variety of flowers including azaleas, roses, and camellias. The large lawn leads to a landing dock that is also used as a diving platform. This secluded part of the property is where the Canepas spend most of their time in spring and summer, sunbathing and playing croquet, or swimming in the refreshing waters of Lake Como.

The elaborate 18th-century Spanish bed is covered with handmade Lombardy lace bedcover and cushions, inset. Spanish antiques are often found in Lombardy's lakeside villas; the region was once occupied by Spain.

A huge 18th-century Italian crystal chandelier, above, illuminates the second-level main salon.

The second-floor hall, with doors opening to lake views, has an Empire flavor—and a chandelier, consoles, and mirrors all dating from the early 1800s, right. The marble floors are not only decorative, but good insulators as well, according to Michele Canepa, who says the second level stays quite warm throughout the winter without heat from radiators.

To emphasize the impact of the villa's exquisite 18th-century frescoes, the Canepas keep the ground-floor salon, left, practically empty. The sofa dates from the early 19th century, the chairs, above, from the 1700s.

Venini vases made from Murano glass are arranged on an 18th-century fireplace in the dining room, above, where the walls are covered with neoclassical frescoes.

EIGHTEENTH-CENTURY VILLA WITH VICTORIAN ANTIQUES

Villa Belvedere has been home to Alessandro Manzoni, the author of *I Promessi Sposi,* composer Vincenzo Bellini, and King George IV of England's younger sons, whose mother, Caroline of Brunswick, lived across the lake on the property that is now Villa d'Este. Built in the late 1700s and enlarged during the following century, the villa is presently owned by Jean-Marc Droulers, the chairman of the Villa d'Este Corporation. He inherited the villa from his father, who bought it several decades earlier.

Jean-Marc Droulers's mother furnished the villa at a leisurely pace, completing it in 1960, and many of the rooms have changed little over the past two and a half decades. "My mother sought to re-create a look that was favored by the Lombardy gentry during the late 1800s," says Mr. Droulers. "It's a somewhat romantic style that used a lot of Napoleon III and Victorian pieces. While there's an abundance of this type of furniture in the house and some of the items are quite good,

Lily ponds with stone fountains, left, are found in many lakeside villas. Villa Belvedere, above, was built in the late 18th century and has had a number of illustrious residents over the years.

185

the whole thing was done inexpensively. My mother is a great bargain hunter, and for years scoured local furniture shops and markets for 19th-century antiques."

The Droulers—Jean-Marc, his mother, his wife, Roberta, and their three children—all live in the villa year-round. "The house is particularly delicious in summer," notes Mr. Droulers, who during warm weather commutes to work by speedboat. "The gardens are full of color, heavily fragrant, and we always have plenty of guests. Villa Belvedere is the type of house that really becomes lovelier when there are lots of people staying in it."

At the edge of the property a wrought-iron-and-glass table and white wood-slat chairs from the 1950s create an informal dining spot, left, cooled by early morning or late afternoon breezes from the lake. The stone balustrade and bench, probably dating from the 1600s, are older than the house. The *putto*, below, is made of Vicenza stone. Nineteenth-century lace curtains, right, from St. Gall, Switzerland, cover living- and dining-room windows.

The Droulers purchased the 19th-century Spanish bed and night table, above, in Madrid. Although Venetian, the mirror, right, matches the ornate style of the Spanish furniture.

The chair and its fabric, left, framed by white cotton curtains in the guest bedroom, date from the Queen Anne period.

HIGH-FASHION VILLA ON MAGGIORE

Gianfranco Ferrè, the Italian fashion designer, is sometimes referred to as the Frank Lloyd Wright of Italian fashion, because of the sophisticated and intricately structured clothes he creates, and the fact that he actually has a university degree in architecture. Although Ferrè never worked as an architect—after graduation he entered the fashion business and quickly became a star—he gets an opportunity to practice a bit of his original craft by designing his own living quarters.

When his search for a small weekend place in 1976 led him to an abandoned Lake Maggiore villa, he bought it even though he knew it would involve a lengthy restoration. But the designer welcomed the opportunity to save the nearly ruined villa and was delighted to find a house only a few hundred feet from the lake he had visited during childhood summers.

A balustraded terrace, left, outside the living room of Gianfranco Ferrè's villa, is an ideal spot for a siesta. The facade, inset right, in ruins when Ferrè saw it in 1976, was restored to the way it looked when the villa was built in the 1850s. The patio, right, large enough only for a small luncheon table, affords a panoramic view of Lake Maggiore.

Ferrè restored the facade to its original mid-1800s appearance, completely re-created the first-floor interior, and rented the upper level. He carved out a large apartment on the ground floor and divided it into two parallel living zones: the living room, dining area, and kitchen, which open onto the garden, and a suite of bedrooms which fill the back of the house. To achieve a warm but streamlined look, Ferrè combined the sofas he designed for B & B Italia with classic modern furniture, items he inherited from his family, and Piedmontese, Venetian, and French antiques. A dedicated traveler, he has brought back decorative objects from his many trips to Morocco, Greece, India, and the Orient, and he's carefully arranged them throughout the apartment.

The designer escapes to his Maggiore home on weekends and invites only the closest of friends and family members for short stays. He likes to give informal luncheons on the lawn, before taking guests out on the lake for a short boat excursion and a swim.

A part of the designer's antique binocular collection is displayed on a living room desk beneath a vase of freshly picked hydrangeas, left. Although Ferrè uses his Lake Maggiore house for relaxation, he did include a large 18th-century Lombard desk, above right, as a workspace in a corner of the living room. He designed the living room's clean-lined, black-lacquer library unit and white sofas, right, as well as many other pieces of furniture in the house.

Another collection, left, includes
19th-century gunpowder and
storage boxes from Bali, southern Italy, and India. White lacquer
paneling covers cabinets and
walls in the small kitchen, top. In
the guest bedroom, above, a Pis-
toletto silk screen dominates one
wall, a long sofa, the other.

PART IV

BY THE MEDITERRANEAN IN SUMMER

The Italian Riviera, The Amalfi Coast, and Sardinia

Italian resorts lining the brilliant Mediterranean Sea are Europe's ultimate summer playgrounds. Their beaches lure a fast-moving and fun-loving crowd—a photogenic mix of international tycoons, cinema stars, artists, English peers, gigolos, bronzed Adonises, and

young beauties, as well as sybarites in search of the perfect tan and a vacation in flawless surroundings. ● Resorts like Positano, Portofino, and Porto Cervo move at a jet-set pace, and their summer residents are usually caught up in an antic social whirl of dusk-to-dawn parties, yacht and disco hopping, and complicated romantic intrigues.

These places have all the potential for being intimidating, but they are not. One expects, almost demands, a certain degree of man-made luxury in areas where the natural beauty is so stunning, where the flowers seem more fragrant, the fruit sweeter, the palm trees more graceful, and the sea more seductive than anywhere else on earth. A playboy's idea of democracy is in effect at all times—three-hundred-foot yachts slip into berths next to fishermen's rowboats, designer boutiques with branches on Milan's Via Montenapoleone and New York's Madison Avenue display cruisewear on the ground floor of waterside *palazzi*  with peeling stucco facades and laundry flapping from windows. The dock hand drinks at the local bar with the shipping magnate and the social arbiter invites any stylish, clever, or beautiful newcomer to partake in the fashionable festivities. ● A typical day in a Mediterranean resort begins slowly. Breakfast is a vaguely remembered concept in Italian summer spots, as many regulars tend to make lunch the first culinary and social event of the day. Served at three or four in the afternoon, lunches are boisterous affairs. New guests drop by with each subsequent course, so that *antipasti* for 4 becomes *gelati* for 20 by dessert time. ● A day at sea or on the beach ends in early evening. Then it's back home to a villa or a magnificent hotel like Portofino's Splendido, Positano's San Pietro, and Porto Cervo hotels Pitrizza or Cala di Volpe for a quick siesta and a

cooling *aperitivo*. Dinners often finish at midnight and are typically followed by several energetic hours on the dance floor of a local discothèque. Weary pleasure seekers head home as the sun rises, hoping to pack in six or seven hours of sleep before the whole routine starts again.

SEASIDE VIEWS

A thin crescent of shorefront land extending from the French border to La Spezia, and a rugged section of the Tyrrhenian seaside beginning in Sorrento and ending in Salerno are the most splendid areas of Italy's 2,500-mile mainland coastline. Both regions—the **Italian Riviera** and the **Amalfi coast**—have rocky landscapes, mountainside dwellings, and roads that wind on cliffs above the sea, but their spirit and style are quite distinct.

The Riviera, particularly the Ligurian part that is southeast of Genoa, is lusher and more colorful than Amalfi. Hans Christian Andersen wrote, "The voyage from Genoa southward along the sea is one of the most beautiful you can make. . . . Views worthy of a painting appear in quick succession. . . ." Citrus, palm,

The Mediterranean coastline offers a way of life that is both sophisticated and simple. At left, open-air lace shops, grand and modest boats, rocky and sandy shores, pastel and deep aqua seas can be found in Italian Mediterranean resorts along the Riviera and the Amalfi coast and in Sardinia. During this century, fishing villages like Portofino, right, tucked into coves and tiny Mediterranean inlets, have become world-famous resorts.

and pine trees blanket hillsides. Narrow *palazzi* rim compact, horseshoe-shaped fishing harbors. A ribbon of endlessly curving road, many parts of which are unprotected by guardrails, tops the vertical cliffs and affords entrancing views of the sea before disappearing into one of a dozen or so tunnels carved out of the mountainside.

Native Ligurians are reserved, hardworking, and notoriously thrifty, but easily accept the *bella vita* life style of their famous resorts. British visitors, including the writers Byron, Shelley, and Oscar Wilde, have had a long romance with the area since the 1800s; the Duke and Duchess of Windsor put the relatively unknown fishing village of Portofino on the map by honeymooning there. Many Riviera towns retain the elegant and somewhat old-fashioned graciousness for which they were famous in the past.

South of Rome, in Campania, you have the sensation of living very much on the edge. The sun is more intense, the landscape rougher—nearby mountains are volcanic—and the *corniche*, particularly along the Amalfi Drive, more harrowing. Traffic is chaotic, street life exuberant. *Amalfitani* have the same boisterous flair for outdoor living as their Neapolitan neighbors. Most natives

are fishermen, but there are also farmers and shepherds; all wear the deep brown tans that come from years of working in the sun.

Seaside towns like Positano, Praiano, and Conca dei Marini are no place for the fainthearted or lazy. To get anywhere—to the beach, your house, your hotel—you are constantly ascending or descending dozens, even hundreds, of stairs.

Amalfi towns have traditionally been inhabited by artists who came to enjoy the sensuous beauty, the glorious views of the Mediterranean, and the raw energy of southern Italy at reasonable prices. While the Amalfi coast has become enormously more developed in the past 20 years and is no longer inexpensive, its original attractions are still potent—and very much a lure for struggling and successful artists, as well as a wide range of visitors from all over the world.

"If we could possess one island, Sardinia, we should want none other," observed British Admiral Horatio Nelson during a cruise of

the Mediterranean in the early 19th century. **Sardinia** was regarded as a rather mysterious place until the 1960s when the Aga Khan and Patrick Guinness bought up a stretch of coastline and began to develop the property into a sleek playground for the rich. While the interior of the island is still rather primitive—a rocky landscape with scrub, wildflowers, the occasional olive tree, and modest farmers' cottages and villages—the Aga Khan's Costa Smeralda is a carefully groomed paradise that was named for the nearby emerald green sea. Here all buildings and villas are designed to blend with the landscape; property owners are told exactly what plants they may grow.

The Costa Smeralda's "capital" is the pristine village of Porto Cervo, made up of a tidy group of low white and rose-colored stucco buildings, tiny immaculate piazzas, restaurants, and discreetly elegant shops catering to a yachtsman's every need. The village is only steps away from the

On a diving platform anchored in the middle of the sea near Portofino, a swimmer and her companion, left, enjoy a little rest. The sheltered harbor of Portofino, inset left, attracts a mix of international yachts, which are moored next to local fishing boats. A Ligurian fisherman, right, heads to his boat in the Portofino harbor.

A vacationer, above, perfects her golden tan near Portofino.

Beach umbrellas and cabanas line a beach in Portofino, above. During weekends in July and the *ferragosto,* or August holidays, Riviera beaches are thoroughly packed, right.

Porto Cervo yacht harbor, filled in the summertime with ocean-going sailboats and mammoth yachts sporting flags from tiny countries known for their lenient tax laws. Located a few kilometers from Porto Cervo are Sardinia's luxury hotels—the Hotel Pitrizza, designed by architect Luigi Vietti, which is famed for its seawater pool built along the rocky shore, and the Hotel Cala di Volpe, created by French architect Jacques Couëlle, which looks like a surrealistic Moorish village.

About a half-hour drive from the Costa Smeralda is another sophisticated, although far less formal area, Porto Rotondo. It was developed by two brothers, the counts Luigi and Niccolò Donà dalle Rose, a few years after the Aga Khan began his work on the Costa Smeralda. Unlike the Costa Smeralda with its international coterie of billionaires, Porto Rotondo is a thoroughly Italian resort, populated by Milanese, Venetians, and Romans, who bring their families to extremely comfortable yet casual villas where they live in bathing suits, attend one another's parties, and keep a low profile.

Hand-painted folkloric motifs decorate the Sardinian chair, left. Most restaurants along the Riviera, like Da Puny in Portofino, above, have an outdoor dining area. Painted stucco *palazzi* line the quay in Portofino, right.

LOCAL COLORS

The Italian coastline is considered by many to be the most beautiful in the world. The transparent waters of the Mediterranean change from dark violet to teal, aqua, or cornflower blue. Huge granite rocks appear to tumble from the shore into the sea, and tiny inlets reveal peaceful fishing villages and strips of sandy beaches. The Riviera's stucco houses, painted raspberry, coral, ochre, and sienna tones, are partially hidden by deep green maritime pines and cypresses. Throughout the spring, almond, peach, and apricot trees blossom with such fullness they seem like oversized bouquets. Red roses and blue hydrangeas color the gardens in summer. Flawless fruit and vegetables are artfully arranged by vendors in local markets: shiny black eggplants; bright red, green, and gold peppers; and deep orange-red tomatoes. Bushels of fragrant basil (this is, after all, the region of pesto) scent the air.

The sharp sun of southern Italy bleaches the yellow, blue, and pink tones of the houses that cluster along the.Amalfi Drive to a watercolor sheerness. White stucco exteriors reflect the strong noonday light. Tiny shops in the center of town offer an assortment of clothing, which is styled for anyone but the shy: aqua, sunflower yellow, cerise, and ruby red skirts, slacks, shawls, and shirts, sometimes adorned with ruffles or flowery embroidery. The flashy clothes look as though they were designed to match the flashy cars that race along the Mediterranean roads. *Gelati* made from fresh berries, peaches, and plums, and cooling drinks like pink Bellinis and crimson Campari and sodas are enjoyed in the late afternoon on terraces overlooking the sea.

Sardinia's dusty rose-colored landscape is frequently austere—but blue skies, white houses wrapped in purple bougainvillea, and shiny sea make the rugged, windswept island seem welcoming.

Vibrantly colored azaleas, bougainvillea, citrus trees, and geraniums, right, flourish in a garden in Positano.

A softly lit pool, above, built at the edge of a mountain slope, stands out against the blue and violet dusk along the Riviera. Elaborate floral patterns decorate a range of fabrics used in native Sardinian costumes, right.

The little ochre-toned Church of St. George in Portofino, left, has a patterned stone pavement and a terrace that affords extensive views of Portofino.

BOATING

Italy's coastline is a boatsman's heaven. There is probably no better way than from a boat to enjoy the Italian seaside with its sheltered coves, sharp fiords, and seaside towns hugging peaceful bays. Small pleasure craft, sleeklined motorboats, and gleaming yachts crisscross the Mediterranean, dock at well-equipped harbors in Porto Cervo, Santa Margherita Ligure, and Sorrento, or drop anchor outside tiny villages like Camogli and San Fruttuoso along the Riviera, and Maiori or Atrani in the Gulf of Salerno. In practically every harbor, you can hire a sailboat, motorboat, or small sailing dinghy. Windsurfing has increased in popularity at major resorts and harbors in Italy in the past decade. Windsurfers sail serenely along scenic coastlines, slipping with ease between fast-moving motorboats and mammoth yachts.

Italy's premier yacht harbor is in Porto Cervo. Its club, the Yacht Club Costa Smeralda, sponsors the Sardinia Cup, an extremely well-publicized sailing regatta for national teams, as well as European championships, like the Gran Premio Offshore Costa Smeralda. International races—the Maxi Yacht Championship and the Swan World Cup—lure a flotilla of ships from around the world. In recent years the Yacht Club Costa Smeralda gained further renown in yachting circles by sponsoring the *Azzurra*, the first 12-meter sailboat built in Italy especially for the America's Cup Challenge.

On Sardinia's Costa Smeralda, the Porto Cervo marina, left and right, is one of the Mediterranean's most popular and glittering yacht basins. With the capacity to dock boats that range in size from 6.5 to 55 meters, the marina attracts a large variety of pleasure craft.

More than 600 yachts can moor at the Porto Cervo marina, and in July and August finding a berth can be quite difficult. Summer holidays and the races and regattas sponsored by the Yacht Club Costa Smeralda cause a near-capacity turnout.

Vacationers don't need to have access to an oceangoing sailboat or yacht to enjoy the Mediterranean. Windsurfing and waterskiing are popular with visitors to the Riviera, Amalfi, and Sardinian resorts. The sails of abandoned wind surfboards, left, create a colorful abstract pattern in the waters off the Costa Smeralda.

SARDINIAN CLOTH

Needlework, weaving, and macramé are among the most popular crafts for Sardinian artisans, who work at home in small towns and hamlets scattered throughout the interior of the island. The artisans produce the bulk of their work during the winter so that they have summers free to sell their wares. They create everything from lavishly embroidered bedspreads, quilts, sheets, and pillowcases to intricately woven rugs and wall hangings. Fabrics are handwoven from linen and wool fibers and yarn that have been dyed and spun by hand.

The most elaborate fabrics are made for the native costumes worn by Sardinians during national holidays and personal celebrations, like baptisms, engagements, and weddings. Women dress in brightly embroidered vests or bolero jackets and long full or pleated skirts. More color can be added to a woman's costume with embroidered shawls and scarves. Men's jerkins are also richly embroidered and worn with short skirts called *bragas* over white linen trousers.

Costume styles, weaving patterns, and fabric, yarn, and thread colors vary from town to town. For example, smoothly woven fabrics are most often found in the small towns of Gadoni and Nule. The popular *pibiònes,* or raised surface, grainy weave is characteristic of Ittiri, Atzara, and San Vito. Geometric, floral, animal, and heraldic designs are found in weaves throughout the island. The influence of the Byzantines, who

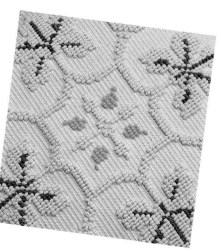

A doll dressed in Sardinian costume, left, is one example of the fine handicrafts produced by two sisters, Rachele and Angela Loche, in their shop in Porto Cervo. A Sardinian woman knots the fringe on a handwoven rug, above. The pillow, right, was hand-loomed to have a raised surface with the popular *pibiònes* effect, so named because it resembles clusters of grapes.

invaded Sardinia, lingers in such oriental motifs as the tree of life, elaborate peacocks and doves, and geometric patterns based on ancient mosaics.

The rich range of Sardinian needlecrafts and fabrics is on display during the summertime in small markets or open-air shops in major Sardinian resorts like Porto Cervo and Porto Rotondo. Recent efforts by Sardinian trade associations are making these lovely products more readily available abroad.

Costumes are somewhat different in each town in Sardinia. Artisans wear garments they've produced, left and above. Yarn used for locally crafted fabrics and embroidery is frequently colored with vegetable dyes, below.

213

TILES

Whether glazed in a single color, intricately patterned, or in rich terra-cotta earth tones, ceramic tiles are an important element in Italian homes. Tiles are used throughout the house, to enliven kitchens, bathrooms, and passageways, and to embellish floors and walls. Easy upkeep makes them a favorite decorative element in seaside vacation houses.

Italy has been producing ceramic tiles since the Middle Ages, when they were used in the homes of nobles and wealthy merchants. Because of the high artistic standards Italians brought to decoration, their tiles soon became famous throughout Europe. Italy today is the world's largest manufacturer of ceramic tiles, with production centers stretching from the Veneto to Sicily.

Ceramic tiles are created from several clays mixed together, then fired at high temperature. An opaque or a transparent glaze, made of melted glass, is fused to the tile during firing for a high-gloss or a matte finish. Unglazed terra-cotta tiles retain the natural tone of the clays. Terra-cotta tiles are enormously popular, particularly in Tuscany, where they are used for pavements outside the house and interior flooring.

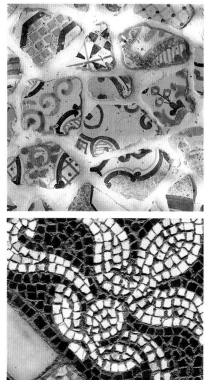

The floral tiles and ceramic wash-basin, hand-painted with the coat of arms of the count Frigeri di Gattatico, left, were made near Amalfi. Savin Couëlle, the architect, used slices of tree trunk and bits of ceramic tile to create unusual pavements, top right and above center right. Elaborate mosaic patterns, found in Venice, above right, inspire contemporary ceramic designs.

SEAFOOD

Italians who live by the Mediterranean look to the sea for their food. Fresh grilled fish, brushed with olive oil and sprinkled with herbs that come from hillsides sloping toward the sea, is a characteristic main course. Regional fish soups are so hearty, though, that many natives and visitors alike willingly forgo a first course of pasta, followed by fish, for the single tasty dish.

Delicious sauces like Liguria's pesto, in its native version a dense blend of basil, parsley, olive oil, pine nuts, garlic, and pecorino cheese, scent the air along the Riviera coast and accent everything from minestrone to spaghetti, ravioli, and gnocchi. Vibrant red *sughi di pomodoro* —tomato sauces made from fresh tomatoes, garlic, olive oil, oregano, and other herbs and spices —complement a wide variety of *amalfitani* pasta dishes. In Sardinia, artichokes, asparagus, and fennel, vegetables that manage to grow on the rocky terrain, are made into delicious sauces for the local varieties of pasta.

Mediterranean breads are tasty and varied. In Liguria, *focaccia,* made with leavened bread dough and seasoned with onion and fennel seeds, is a favorite of everyone from schoolchildren to sophisticated chefs. A popular Ligurian Christmas gift, *pandolce,* the region's version of *panettone,* is a sweet bread made with sultanas, raisins, candied citron, pumpkin, pine nuts, and fennel seeds. Breads are shaped into large loaves or religious or natural motifs for holidays, or made into light, delicate wafers. In the south of Italy, there's an enormous variety of tasty pizzas and *calzoni,* doughy turnovers filled with mozzarella and prosciutto, which vacationers in Amalfi can look forward to sampling.

Pecorino, the hard sheep's milk cheese, is popular in both Liguria and Sardinia and is sometimes used in place of *parmigiano* to season pasta sauces. In the Amalfi area, the fresh *mozzarella di bufala,* sold either as a braid or in oval or rounded shapes, appears at most every *pranzo* during the summer. Desserts in Mediterranean regions tend to be light and simple—a piece of fruit, a *macedonia* of berries, or some nuts and a handful of grapes.

Along the Italian Mediterranean coast in summer, pasta is often seasoned with fresh vegetables. The spaghetti with artichoke and asparagus is frequently served at the San Pietro Hotel in Positano.

Bernard Bohn

SPAGHETTI ALLA SAN PIETRO

- **1 medium artichoke**
- **½ lemon**
- **4 tablespoons unsalted butter**
- **3 tablespoons extra virgin olive oil**
- **2 garlic cloves, crushed**
- **8 asparagus spears, trimmed**
- **½ pound spaghetti**
- **2 tablespoons minced Italian parsley**
- **1 teaspoon salt**
- **½ teaspoon freshly ground pepper Sprigs of Italian parsley, for garnish**
- **½ cup freshly grated parmesan cheese**

Cut the stem off the artichoke; rub the cut surface with lemon half. Bend back and pull off the tough outer leaves. Cut off the top third of the artichoke. With scissors, snip off any thorns from the tops of the remaining leaves.

Squeeze the lemon juice into a medium saucepan of salted water. Bring to a boil, add the trimmed artichoke and cook, covered, until the bottom is easy to pierce with a knife, 15 to 25 minutes. Drain; set aside and keep warm.

Meanwhile, in a small saucepan, combine the butter, oil, and garlic over low heat. Sauté until the garlic is soft but not browned, about 10 minutes.

In a skillet of boiling salted water, cook the asparagus until crisp-tender, about 3 minutes. Drain, cover, and keep warm.

Cook the pasta in boiling water until just al dente, about 10 minutes. Drain and turn into a large heated bowl. Reserving 1 tablespoon of the garlic sauce, strain the remaining sauce over the pasta; toss to coat. Add the minced parsley, salt, and pepper, and toss well.

Spread apart the inner leaves of the artichoke and scoop out the choke. Arrange the pasta on a large platter and place the artichoke in the center. Arrange asparagus spears around it in a circle, like the spokes of a wheel. Pour the reserved garlic sauce into the center of the artichoke.

Garnish the platter with parsley and split the artichoke in half at the table. Pass the parmesan separately.

Serves 2

SCAMPI A CARTOCCIO

Shrimp en Papillote

- **1½ pounds linguine or spaghetti**
- **3 tablespoons olive oil**
- **4 tablespoons unsalted butter**
- **1 garlic clove, minced**
- **¼ teaspoon dried hot red pepper flakes**
- **2 pounds large shrimp, peeled, deveined, and halved lengthwise**
- **2 large tomatoes, cored, seeded, and chopped (about 1 cup)**
- **2 tablespoons Cognac or brandy**
- **Pinch of salt**
- **¾ cup dry white wine**
- **¼ cup minced Italian parsley**

Preheat the oven to 400°F.

Cook the pasta in boiling water until almost al dente but not yet tender to the bite. Drain very well. Coat the pasta lightly with 1 tablespoon of the olive oil to keep the strands from sticking together. Set aside.

In a large skillet or sauté pan, melt the butter with the remaining 2 tablespoons olive oil over moderate heat. Add the garlic and red pepper flakes and sauté until the garlic is softened, about 2 minutes. Add the shrimp and tomatoes and toss to coat. Pour in the Cognac and ignite it. Cook, shaking the pan, until the flames subside. Season with the salt and add the wine to the skillet. Cook, stirring from time to time, until the shrimp are just opaque, 3 to 5 minutes.

Using a slotted spoon, remove the shrimp to a bowl. Pour any liquid that drains off back into the skillet. Place the skillet over high heat and boil until reduced to about ¾ cup and thickened somewhat.

Meanwhile, stack up six 18 x 12-inch sheets of parchment paper. Cut the sheets into wide ovals. Lightly brush each sheet of parchment with olive oil, reaching to within 1½ inches of the edges.

Divide the pasta into six equal portions. Place one "nest" of pasta on the right side of each parchment oval. Divide the shrimp over the mounds of pasta. When the cooking liquid is reduced, stir in the parsley. Spoon some of the cooking liquid over each portion of shrimp.

Fold the left side of the parchment over each serving and crimp the edges several times to create a tightly sealed package.

Place the parchment packages on a jelly-roll pan. Bake for 10 to 15 minutes, until the parchment is puffed and lightly browned. Place one package on each dinner plate and slit open with a sharp knife.

Serves 6

Dining all'aperto in small trattorias near the beach is just one of the delights the Italian Riviera has to offer during the spring and summer. The Da Puny restaurant, above, in Portofino is a favorite with both local residents and visitors.

Bernard Bohn

Scampi a cartoccio, **a mixture of langoustines or jumbo shrimp, basil, and linguini, left, as it is served at Positano's San Pietro Hotel. A homemade lemon liqueur, above, offers a cooling refreshment on hot summer afternoons.**

PIZZA RUSTICA

from Antico Francischiello on the Amalfi Coast

Dough

- 2 cups all-purpose flour
- 2 tablespoons sugar
- 1 teaspoon grated lemon zest
  Pinch of salt
- 8 tablespoons (¼ pound) cold unsalted butter, cut into bits
- 2 egg yolks
- 4 to six tablespoons ice water

Filling

- 3 whole eggs
- ½ cup heavy cream
- 1½ cups ricotta cheese
- 8 ounces mozzarella cheese, shredded (2 cups)
- 2 tablespoons freshly grated parmesan cheese
- 6 ounces prosciutto, minced
- 2 tablespoons raisins
  Freshly ground pepper

Dough: In a food processor, combine the flour, sugar, zest, and salt. Sprinkle the butter over the top. Pulse on and off until the mixture is coarsely chopped and mixed. Add the egg yolks and 3 tablespoons of the ice water, and pulse until the mixture forms a rough dough. Add more ice water, 1 tablespoon at a time, as necessary, until the mixture is moist enough to gather into a ball.

Wrap the dough in plastic wrap and refrigerate for at least 1 hour.

Filling: Preheat the oven to 375°.

In a large bowl, beat the eggs with the cream. Add the ricotta and beat until well combined. Add the mozzarella and parmesan and mix until well moistened and coated with the egg. Stir in the prosciutto and raisins and season with pepper to taste. Set aside.

On a lightly floured surface, roll out the dough into a circle about 14 inches in diameter. Fit the pastry into a 10-inch deep-dish pizza pan or pie plate. Crimp the edges.

Pour the filling into the pie-crust. Bake for 50 to 55 minutes, until the top is golden brown all over.

Remove from the oven and cool on a wire rack. Cut into wedges and serve at room temperature.

Serves 6 to 8

LEMON LIQUEUR

from La Pigna in Capri

- 8 lemons
- 1 liter 90-proof vodka
- 3 cups sugar

Wash the lemons and dry them. Using a swivel vegetable peeler, remove the zest from the lemons in strips, taking care to strip off only the outer yellow peel and none of the white pith.

Open the vodka bottle and stuff the zest into the neck of the bottle. Seal and shake to mix the zest with the vodka. Set aside for 1 week.

In a saucepan, combine the sugar with 4 cups water. Bring to a boil over high heat, stirring to melt the sugar. Set the sugar syrup aside to cool to room temperature.

Pour the cooled sugar syrup into a large pitcher. Add the lemon-flavored vodka and stir to combine very well. Line a funnel with a double thickness of dampened cotton cheesecloth. Strain the liqueur through the cheesecloth into two 1-liter bottles. Seal tight. Set aside to develop for 15 days.

Place the bottles of liqueur in the freezer and chill until very cold. Serve in chilled glasses.

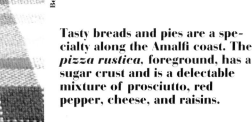

Tasty breads and pies are a specialty along the Amalfi coast. The *pizza rustica*, foreground, has a sugar crust and is a delectable mixture of prosciutto, red pepper, cheese, and raisins.

Bernard Bohn

SEASIDE HOUSES, TERRACES, AND GARDENS

Most Italian seaside houses were constructed during the last two hundred years. *Palazzi* bordering the harbors and shores of the Italian peninsula date from the 19th century; villas high in the mountains were built after World War II, and those along Sardinia's Costa Smeralda and Porto Rotondo originated in the 1960s. In desirable spots like Portofino and Positano, new construction and the alteration of existing structures are now prohibited by the local preservation group.

Since most real estate along the Riviera and the Amalfi coast is in the mountains, suitable property for building has always been at a premium. Unless they are quite small, villas tend to ramble down the rocky slopes of the steep seaside terrain. Green shutters and tiny white or black wrought-iron balconies decorate the brightly colored stucco facades of Riviera houses. Villas of the Amalfi coast have low flat roofs and arch-trimmed porticoes reminiscent of houses in southern Spain and northern Morocco.

In contrast to the mainland shoreline, Sardinia has an abundance of coastal property that is flat. The Aga Khan hired three noted architects, Jacques Couëlle, his son Savin Couëlle, and Luigi Vietti, to develop the virgin territory with buildings that would harmonize with the landscape. The Couëlles proposed a "geobiologic" architecture that treats the houses and terrain as an indissoluble unit. In a Couëlle villa, walls are often curved around preexisting rock formations.

Luigi Vietti's architecture is more classic, but he, too, is a master at building houses that barely seem to intrude upon their environment. Constructed from local stone, and topped with roofs of native juniper wood, his houses are covered with a profusion of flowers, shrubs, and creeper vines that make them hard to detect from the sea, the road, or the air.

Mainland villas closest to the water are usually casual, with colorfully patterned ceramic tile floors, stucco interior walls, stone stairs, white canvas-covered sofas and chairs. Houses tend to become more formal in the mountains, and include antique furniture and carpets, and fabric-lined walls, particularly if they are occupied beyond the month of August.

In Sardinia, the look is sumptuous yet contemporary. Most houses have an outdoor as well as indoor living and dining area with granite banquettes and tables carved from surrounding rock, and furniture, upholstery fabrics, and tiles that are locally made. Bedrooms are sparsely decorated, but the white netting draped around beds adds a romantic touch.

FORMER RECTORY IN POSITANO

The Spreaficos chose Positano as a retirement spot because of its mild winter climate, its opportunities for sailing, and their many friends who lived year-round in the area. They bought a 17th-century rectory perched high on a mountain with striking views of the town, and converted it into a home filled with Italian antiques and artifacts collected on trips all over the world.

Inspired by the many buildings in Positano with an Arabic flavor, the Spreaficos incorporated some details from Moroccan villas into the redesign of the rectory. The semienclosed entryway, with its graceful fountains, shrubs, and stucco walls rimmed with built-in stone benches, calls to mind Moorish dwellings. Inside the house, large open arches divide the various rooms, which all have floors covered in brightly colored decorative tiles.

Jade plants, palm trees, and lemon arbors flourish in the sunny garden. One part of the property also has a one-lane swimming pool.

The villa's entranceway, right, was inspired by Moorish dwellings, where interior courtyards often have plants and shrubs, cooling fountains, left, tiled floors, and white stucco walls. The second floor of the villa, a former rectory, opens to a large terrace, inset right. Adjacent to the house is a church built in the 15th century.

Brightly patterned tiles made in the region add an informal touch to the 18th-century antique-filled living room, left. Because beaches are often crowded in the summertime and there are many long flights of stone steps down from their mountainside house, the Spreaficos installed a one-lane lap pool for exercise at the edge of their garden overlooking Positano, overleaf.

Rosita and Giancarlo Spreafico, above, live in Positano year-round. A framed 17th-century Italian fan, right, hangs on a living room wall. The Spreaficos display the hats they collect in a small bedroom, far right.

CONVERTED FACTORY WITH TERRACES

The large waterside villa in Conca dei Marini was formerly a rope factory until a prominent French family bought and redesigned it for use as a vacation home. Spanish architect Julio la Fuente oversaw the restoration, merging the factory building with its adjacent small stone house, which once belonged to Coco Chanel.

To satisfy his clients' love for outdoor living, La Fuente created two enormous terraces on either side of the living room that dominates the villa's top floor. One of the terraces, shaded by a bamboo roof and swept by sea breezes, is an ideal place for an afternoon siesta. The other terrace, thickly planted with Mediterranean shrubs and flowers, is used as an al fresco dining area.

The villa is furnished primarily with contemporary pieces. La Fuente chose a white, blue, and yellow color scheme to complement the tones of the sea and sky. An art studio, main and service kitchens, bedrooms, and guest rooms are located on levels below the main salon. Most rooms have panoramic views of the sea.

Accessible only by boat or by a long walk down dozens of flights of stone stairs, the villa affords the owners the privacy they seek. It is such a tranquil spot that First Lady Jacqueline Kennedy came here in the afternoons during an Italian holiday to escape the paparazzi who stalked her.

The easiest way to approach houses built on rocky cliffs along the Amalfi coast is often by boat, top left. The former net and rope factory, above left, built in the late 18th century, was converted by a Paris-based family into a spacious seaside house. Trimming the rugged terrain, the sea glitters in the midday sun, left.

The floor-to-ceiling doors of the living room and bedrooms open onto terraces overlooking the Gulf of Salerno, left.

229

To add interest to the white stucco, architect Julio la Fuente embedded stone from the region in the arched passageway leading to the terrace, left, and the walls off the main living room. The spacious living room's vaulted ceiling, right, is original to the house. The ceramic plates on the coffee table are from Amalfi, as are the yellow sofa and chairs. Eighteenth-century floor tiles, below and right, were found in a Neapolitan palace.

A large terrace, left and above,
and a smaller one, top, flank
either side of the main-floor
living room. The large terrace
has a bamboo roof and bamboo
furniture covered with canvas
cushions and pillows that were
embroidered in the region. The
smaller terrace contains plants
and trees that will later be rooted
in the garden and is a favorite
spot for breakfasts and lunches.

MULTILEVEL VILLA ON THE AMALFI DRIVE

The Amalfi area always had a special meaning for the late Count Giorgio Frigeri and his Austrian-born wife, Marion. They had met at a mutual friend's house near Amalfi when Marion came to see the town where her father had hidden during World War II. They both adored the beauty and leisurely rhythm of the region, and when film producer Giorgio Frigeri retired, they decided to buy a vacation home along the Amalfi Drive.

During a seven-year period, the Frigeris oversaw the conversion of the tiny cliffside farmer's house in Praiano into a gracious villa. Because of the sloped and rocky terrain, the house had to be built on five floors. The entrance hall is at street level; the living and dining room, kitchen and guest suites, and master bedroom are arranged on the three floors below it. The fifth and lowest level is a *cantina,* or wine cellar.

The Frigeri house, like many other villas along the Amalfi coast, was built on a rocky cliff that descends toward the sea. Often these houses are hidden from view by vegetation or, as in the case of the Frigeri villa, have roofs that are almost level with the road. An antique bell, inset, stands out against the stark white stone and stucco roof.

Although the villa was planned to be a vacation home, the couple eventually decided to live in it year-round. Marion Frigeri furnished the house with a mixture of French, Austrian, Italian, and English antiques. Pink, blue, and white fabrics and flowers lend colorful accents.

Wrapped in shrubs and trees, the villa looks like it is part of the mountainside. But views from the living room terraces are sweeping and quite romantic in the evening. Tiny dots of light from houses along the shore and in the mountains, from boats anchored at sea and docked in the harbor, blink in the dark of a Mediterranean night.

Narrow stone steps, typical of the Amalfi region, flank the side of the house and lead to the garden, above. The Frigeris created an outdoor dining terrace, which overlooks the garden and the sea. Countess Frigeri adds flowers picked from the garden to her table setting, right.

236

The terrace, lined with the same blue tiles that were used for interior flooring, overlooks the Mediterranean, above. The contemporary wrought-iron rocking chair contrasts with the antique capital found in the area.

A wrought-iron grille and ivy vines frame a dining room window, left. The terra-cotta vase is from the 18th century.

237

TOWN HOUSE IN MEDIEVAL VILLAGE

Beppe Modenese, the director of Milano Collezioni, the group that organizes the Italian ready-to-wear fashion shows, wanted a seaside house in a relatively unknown town, where he could enjoy complete peace and relaxation during the month of August. He found an old *frantoio,* a little structure that housed the remnants of an olive oil press, in Monte Marcello, a village inhabited by five hundred people, near the gulf of La Spezia at the southern end of the Riviera. With the help of interior designer Piero Pinto, he transformed the nearly ruined building —only exterior walls were standing—into a comfortable four-story vacation house.

Planters and urns of geraniums surround the entrance to the Monte Marcello town house, left, which was once the site of the village olive oil press. A wrought-iron gate, above, separates the back of the town house from the medieval village's tiny main street. The blue and white ceramic bench, below, was produced by Portuguese artisans re-creating an early 18th-century design.

Since the town house is narrow, each floor has only one or two rooms. A kitchen and informal dining area, covered in blue Portuguese tiles that create a rustic Mediterranean feeling, make up the ground floor. The living areas on the second level are joined by an open arched doorway and include dramatically shaped black sofas, sculptures, and slate tables, which stand out against the white stucco walls and the white ceramic floor tiles that were chosen for their special luminosity.

A slate terrace outside the living room, rimmed with a pink stucco banquette, is the perfect setting for cocktails at twilight. There one frequently finds house guests and a dozen or so friends, who, like Beppe Modenese, were enchanted by and bought apartments or houses in the tiny medieval village.

Open, arched passageways subdivide the main level into various sitting rooms, left. Piero Pinto chose a black and white scheme for the living room, right. He used white walls and ceramic tiles as a backdrop for the furniture he designed. The zebra carpet is from Kenya.

PORTOFINO MOUNTAIN HOUSE

The villa was several hundred meters above the sea in Portofino, and the new owners, a family from Milan who needed a house for business entertaining as well as personal use, wanted an elegantly informal home. With the help of their architect, Filippo Perego, they created an updated version of a Riviera summer house that might

Like most villas in Portofino, this mountainside house, top, is covered by trees and shrubs which offer beauty and privacy. Because the roads leading to houses in the mountains above Portofino are so small, a minivan, above, is the only vehicle permitted.

In the cypress-rimmed Riviera garden, a marble fountain filled with flowers, left, receives a late-afternoon watering. An elaborate wicker chair with a locally crafted pillow, right, is sometimes moved to a terrace outside the master bedroom.

TRAVELER'S GUIDE

Part of the joy and excitement of visiting Italy is discovering the special places to stay, enjoying the restaurants that capture the flavors of the region, and seeing the memorable sites. The following hotels, restaurants, and places to visit for each region featured in *Italian Country* were recommended by people who have homes in the area or vacation there frequently. Although a number of the listings are well-known favorites, most reflect the enthusiastic and highly personal opinion that a native or well-traveled friend might give you. Distances are quoted in kilometers—1 kilometer = .62 mile.

Hotels are designated luxury (L), first class (F or F+), or moderately priced (M); restaurants, expensive (E), moderate (M), or inexpensive (I). Unless otherwise noted, restaurants specialize in regional dishes. A list of rental agencies for houses in Italy is also included.

Shops for antiques, bed and bath linens, fabrics, woodcrafts, and so on are organized under region and by specialty in Italy, and under London and regions and by specialty in the United Kingdom. Antiques shops in Italy generally carry furniture from the area unless otherwise indicated and antiques dating anywhere from the Renaissance to the late 19th century. If an antiques shop specializes in a certain period, that has been indicated, too.

Research assistant: Stefania Vimercati. UK research by Jan Cumming
Maps: Oliver Williams

RENTING A HOUSE
In Italy

The Best in Tuscany
Via Ugo Foscolo 72
50124 Florence   055/223064
Contact: Count Girolamo and Countess Simonetta Brandolini d'Adda. Small, medium, and large villas, as well as apartments in Positano, Tuscany, Umbria, the Veneto, Florence, and Venice.

Italian Properties
Piazza dell'Incontro 2
06012 Città di Castello
(PG)   075/8554208
Selection of rental villas and apartments, villas for sale, *case coloniche* for refurbishing. When contacting from the UK, phone 075/8559597 (14 Via Marconi).

Tuscany, Umbria, Venice Rental Consultants

Borgo Pinti 82
50125 Florence   055/6812185
Castles, *palazzi*, villas, and some apartments in areas indicated above.

In the United Kingdom

Citalia
50/51 Conduit Street
London W1R 9FB
01-134 3814
Villas and apartments for rent throughout Italy.

Interhome
383 Richmond Road
Twickenham TW1 2EF
01-891 1294
Villas and apartments for rent throughout Italy.

Italian Properties
Old Telephone Exchange
Eckington
Worcestershire WR10 3AP

0386 750133
Villas for sale in Umbria and Tuscany border.
For rent, 0905 60327.

Italien Tours-Vacanze Italiene
22 Church Rise
London SE23
01-291 1450
Villas, farmhouses and apartments for rent in Tuscany and Umbria.

The Magic of Italy
47 Shepherds Bush Green
London W12 8PS
01-743 9900

Villas and apartments for rent throughout Italy, plus the option of traveling on the Orient-Express.

Villas Italia
227 Shepherds Bush Road
London W6 7AS
01-740 9988
Villas and apartments for rent throughout Italy.

For further information and travel details contact the Italian State Tourist Office,
1 Princes Street,
London W1R 8AY, 01-408 1254.

THE COUNTRYSIDE
Tuscany

HOTELS

Grand hotels are located in historic villas like Lucca's Villa la Principessa, once the home of the Duke of Lucca, and Villa San Michele, designed by Michelangelo. Small inns like the Villa Casalecchi, the Certosa di Maggiano, the Locanda dell'Amorosa are well situated for exploring the countryside.

CASTELLINA IN CHIANTI: Villa Casalecchi. 0577/740240 (F+)
FIESOLE: Villa San Michele. Via Doccia 4. 055/59451 (L)
LUCCA: Villa la Principessa. Massa Pisana. 0583/370037 (L)
SIENA: Certosa di Maggiano. Strada di Certosa 82. 0577/288180 (F+)
SINALUNGA: Locanda dell'Amorosa. 0577/679479 (M)

RESTAURANTS

All the restaurants listed feature hearty, country-style cooking with the exception of Il Cibreo and Biribisso in Florence, which offer lighter and more modern versions of traditional Tuscan dishes. For the famous *bistecca alla fiorentina,* go to Sostanza and the Locanda dell'Amorosa.

CASTELLINA IN CHIANTI: Pestello. 0577/740215 (M)
Antica Trattoria la Torre. 0577/740236 (M)
CETONA: La Frateria di Padre Eligio. 0577/749483 (M)
GAIOLE IN CHIANTI: Badia a Coltibuono al Giannete. 0577/749424 (M)
Castello di Spalatenna. 0577/749483 (M)
FLORENCE: Biribisso. Via dell'Albero 28/R. 055/293180 (M)
Il Cibreo, Via dei Macci, 118. 055/667394 (M)
Da Ganino Hosteria. Piazza Cimatori, 4/R. 055/212125. (M)
Sostanza, Via del Porcellana 25R.
Vecchia Bettola, viale Ludovico Ariosto, 32. 055/224158 (M)
LUCCA: Buca di San Antonio. Via della Cerva 1. 0583/55881 (M–E)
Solferino. Hamlet of San Marcario in Piano. 0583/59118 (M)

265

MONTALCINO. La Cucina di Edgardo. 0577/848232 (M)

MONTEFOLLONICO: La Chiusa. Via della Madonnina 88. 0577/669668 (M)

MONTEPULCIANO: Pulcino. 0578/757905 (M–E)

SINALUNGA: Locanda dell'Amorosa. 0577/679497 (M)

EXCURSIONS
Chianti Road to Siena: Pastoral Views/Chianti Wine Estates

See map, page 265. Travel by car. Allow 1–2 days for the approximately 100 km. trip from Florence to Siena, depending on the number of wine estates you plan to see. To schedule visits to the major wine estates like Castello di Brolio, Castello di Cacchiano, or Badia a Coltibuono (or others in the region), contact the Consorzio Chianti Classico in Florence, 055/229351. Travel from Florence along S 222 through the towns of Greve, Montefioralle, Panzano, Castellina in Chianti, turn east on S 429 to Gaiole in Chianti, then via S 408 to Siena (S 484 if you visit Castello di Brolio).

SHOPPING

Florence is world famous for its numerous street markets—the Mercato di San Lorenzo, near the Church of San Lorenzo, for clothing and shoes; the Mercato della Pulci, Piazza dei Ciompi, for an eclectic assortment of low-priced antiques, books, and fabrics; the Mercato Nuovo for straw and leather items.

Antiques markets are common in Tuscany. In Florence, for instance, the antiques market is held every Thursday morning in the Piazza Tasso, while there's an antiques market in Lucca's Piazza San Martino on the third Saturday and Sunday of every month.

Antiques

Most farmhouse owners say they furnish their houses with pieces found at local markets. For those without the time or inclination for flea market shopping, Florence has a number of excellent antiques shops, usually located along the Via Borgognissanti, the Via dei Fossi, Via Maggio, and Via Tornabuoni. The Via Toscanella and Borgo Tegolaio have a number of *botteghe*, local shops that take the place

of covered markets, filled with artisan-crafted and rustic furniture. The following stores offer a variety of antiques.

FLORENCE

Bartolozzi, Guido & Figlio
Via Maggio 18/R
Fifteenth-century Tuscan, as well as Venetian and Genovese furniture.

Banco 22
Via del Sole. 055/280239
Nineteenth- and 20th-century furniture from northern Italy.

Luzzetti
Borgo San Jacopo 28/A. 055/211232
Renaissance furniture from Tuscany.

Sandro Morelli Antichità
Via Maggio 51/R. 055/282789
Sixteenth- and 17th-century Tuscan furniture, 13th–16th-century sculpture.

Pratesi
Borgo SS Apostoli
Seventeenth- and 18th-century Tuscan furniture.

Bed and Bath Linens

FLORENCE

Baroni
Via Tornabuoni 8/R. 055/210562
Custom-made linens, towels.

Caponi
Borgo Ognissanti 12. 055/213668
Hand-embroidered linens, bedspreads, and antique lace cushions.

Mazzoni
Via Orsanmichele 14/R. 055/215153
Bed and table linens, bath accessories, robes, silk sheets.

Pratesi
Lungarno A. Vespucci 8/10R
Plain and hand-embroidered linens and bath accessories.

Ceramics

Most of the following stores take orders for individualized patterns for dishes, bowls, and vases. An average of 30–60 days is needed for completion. Mailings to the United States are easily arranged.

FLORENCE

Riccardo Barthel
Via dei Fossi 11/R. 055/283683
Variety of antique patterns.

Ceramiche Calzaiuoli
Via Calzaiuoli 8. 055/262763

Reproductions of antique Tuscan, Deruta, Della Robbia ceramics.

Davim Regali
Via Tornabuoni 101/R
Contemporary tiles and designer ceramics.

Ceramiche Menegatti
Piazza del Pesce 2. 055/215202
Tuscan faience, reproductions of Della Robbia plates.

MONTELUPO

Ceramiche Bellucci
Corso Garibaldi 71. 0571/51022
Sixteenth- and 17th-century Tuscan patterns.

MONTESPERTOLI

Leona Riproduzioni di Antiche Ceramiche
Via Virginio 218. 0571/671238
Tuscan motifs for vases, plates, bowls.

Fabrics

FLORENCE

Antico Setificio Fiorentino
Via della Vigna Nuova 97
Taffeta, damask, velvets, passementerie.

Cesari
Via Tornabuoni 2. 055/263846
Velvets, brocades patterned with Florentine Renaissance motifs. Hand-loomed, custom-made fabrics.

Dino Levi Antiques
Via Maggio 53/R. 055/212815
Antique Italian embroidered fabric, costumes, and altar pieces from the 18th century.

Lisio Tessuti d'Arte
Via dei Fossi 45
Antique woven silk fabrics inspired by classic paintings.

Rubelli
Via Tornabuoni 3/R. 055/212520
Lampas, damask, printed silks with antique patterns.

Silvi
Via dei Tavolini 5
Wide selection of trim and passementerie.

Stationery

FLORENCE

Pneider
Piazza Signoria 13/R and
Via Tornabuoni 76/R
Fine writing paper, address books, appointment books, calendars.

SIENA

Il Papiro
Via di Città 37
Writing paper and cards with Guelph/Ghibelline and other antique motifs.

Umbria

HOTELS
The best hotels in Umbria are country inns. All of the inns listed below are extremely restful and their restaurants are noted for excellent food.
ORVIETO: La Badia. 0763/90359 (F)
TODI: San Valentino Hotel and Sporting Club. 075/884103 (F)

TORGIANO: Le Tre Vaselle. 075/982447 (F)

RESTAURANTS
Umbrian cuisine, like Tuscan, is simple, tasty, and hearty. The region is known for its truffles, which are served in many varieties in Umbrian restaurants in the fall, most notably at Ta-

verna del Lupo and Il Tartufo. Game is a specialty at Alla Fornace di Maestro Giorgio and Il Cacciatore.

AREZZO: Buca di San Francesco. Piazza San Francesco 1. 0575/23271 (M)

CITTÀ DI CASTELLO: Il Bersaglio. 075/8535534 (M)

CORCIANO (Perugia): Osteria dell' Olmo. 075/799140 (M–E)

GUBBIO: Alla Fornace di Maestro Giorgio. Via Maestro Giorgio 2. 075/9275740 (M)

Taverna del Lupo. Via Ansidei 21. 075/9274368 (E)

ORVIETO: La Badia. 0763/ 90359 (M)

SPELLO: Il Cacciatore. Via Giulia 62. 0742/65114 (M)

SPOLETO: Il Tartufo. Piazza Garibaldi. 0743/40236 (M–E)

Tric-Trac. Piazza del Duomo. 0743/44592 (M–E)

TORGIANO: Le Tre Vaselle. Via Garibaldi 48. 075/982447 (M)

EXCURSIONS
Medieval Hill Towns of Umbria

See map, page 266. Plan 2–3 days to travel leisurely by car. Start in Gubbio, then travel to Perugia, Assisi, Spello, detour through Bevagna, Foligno, Trevi, Spoleto, Todi, and finish in Orvieto. About 200 km. Roads are generally good. Gas stations closed for better part of afternoons and on Sundays in many small towns.

SHOPPING

As in Tuscany, antiques markets are regular events in Umbria. But the one favored by the region's farmhouse owners is the Arezzo market held in the old center of town the first Saturday and Sunday of every month.

Furniture fairs are also commonly held in Umbrian cities each weekend. Check with your local concierge or the Umbrian Tourist Board in Perugia, Corso Vanucci 30, 075/24841, or Via Mazzini 9, 075/50217. The Mostra dell'Antiquariato, the national antiques show, is held in Todi in March and in Assisi in April and May.

Ceramics

In addition to the stores listed below, those interested in Umbrian ceramics should visit the towns of Orvieto and Gualdo Tadino, which have numerous ceramics shops lining the streets in the center of town. Individualized patterns for dishes, bowls, and vases can be ordered from most of the stores listed below. Mailings to the United States are easily arranged. About 30–60 days are needed for completion of a project.

DERUTA

Grazia C&C Maioliche
Via Tiberina
Antique patterns, custom orders.

Fratelli Mari
Via Tiberina 230
Motifs inspired by Raphael.

GUBBIO

Rampini
Via dei Consoli 66
Typical *Eugubina* (from Gubbio) ceramics, frequently black.

Fabrics

CITTÀ DI CASTELLO

La Tela Umbra
Piazza Costa
Handwoven linens. Weaving lessons in summer.

LAGO TRASIMENO

Semolesti, Isola Maggiore
Handmade lace.

PERUGIA

Ceccucci
Corso Vannucci 38
Range of handwoven fabrics.

SPOLETO

M. L. Bastiani Baragli
Via San Antonio
Laces inspired by antique patterns.

Maestro Raphael
(hamlet of S. Chiddo). 0743/42747
Embroidered pillows, sheets.

Woodcrafts

ORVIETO

Gualviero Michelangeli
Via Albaini 1
Dolls, rocking horses, environmental sculptures.

G. Mascherini
Corso Cavour
Hand-carved puppets, Pinocchios.

PERUGIA

Baciocchi
Via Maesta delle Volpi 8

THE MOUNTAINS
Cortina d'Ampezzo

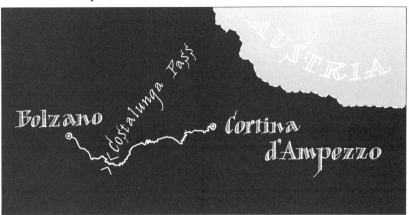

HOTELS

The grandest hotels in Italian mountain resorts are rarely located on the slopes. While convenient to skiing facilities, hotels may be situated in the heart of town, or on a hillside that affords outstanding views.

Cristallo. Via Menardi 42. 0436/4281 (L)

De la Poste, Piazza Roma 14. 0436/4271 (F)

RESTAURANTS

Dishes from the Veneto and Trentino/Alto Adige are served in Cortina d'Ampezzo. Il Camineto and Il Meloncino located near Cortina's ski runs are favorite choices for lunch.

Il Cristallo. Hotel Cristallo. 0436/4281 (M–E)

De la Poste. 0436/4271 (M–E)

Lago Scin. Strada Statale. 0436/2391 (M)

Il Meloncino (hamlet of Gilardon, foot of Socrepes slope). 0436/61043 (M)

Rifugio di Bona. 0436/60294 (M)

Tivoli Restaurant. Lacedel 34. 0436/66400 (M)

El Toula. Via Ronco 123. 0436/3339 (E)

Pastry Shops and Cafés

Go to Embassy and Lovat for Dobos and Sacher Torte and coffee; Pasticceria Artigiana, Via Cesare Battista 54, for exquisite cakes and pastries. Geri's Enoteca, Via del Mercato 5, is a popular wine bar.

SKI INFORMATION

Cortina has a ski school in the center of town. Group and private ski lessons for downhill and cross-country are available. The Cortina Card plan provides discounts on lodging and ski facilities from early January to April. Ski passes allow access to all facilities. Ski rental: Olympia on the Corso Italia.

EXCURSIONS
Transdolomitic Road

See map, above. One day by car, 133 km. from Bolzano to Costalunga Pass to Cortina d'Ampezzo. One of the Dolomites' most beautiful roads.

SHOPPING

In the center of downtown Cortina there's a market each Thursday and Friday with everything from wrought-iron objects to dried flowers.

Antiques

Antichità Red & Figli srl.
Corso Italia 220. 0436/3762.

El Touladel
1 Via Col. 0436/66219
Via XXIX Maggio. 04367/61308

E. Ruffier
11 Via della Vittoria Dolonne.
0436/842562

Costumes

(Ampezzani and Tirolese)
Giacobbi
Corso Italia 101. 0436/4308.

Ghedina Zuccaro
Corso Italia 101. 0436/4308

Fabrics

Antonio Tessuti
Corso Italia 127. 0436/61301

Arcarosas
Via XXIV Maggio 18. 0436/60288

Moessmer
Corso Italia 160. 0436/61301

Woodcrafts

Artigianato Artistico Ampezzano
Corso Italia/Palazzo del Vecchio
Municipio. 0436/3527

Art House di G. Gasperi
Corso Italia 96. 0436/3898

Piccolori Giorgio
Via Alvera 53. 0436/61997

Flowers

(dried mountain floral bouquets)
Chalet des Edelweiss
11014 Entroubles (hamlet of Vachery)
0165/78100

Woodcrafts

Courmayeur l'Artisanat
11020 St. Christophe (hamlet of
Grand Chemin). 0165/3631

Courmayeur

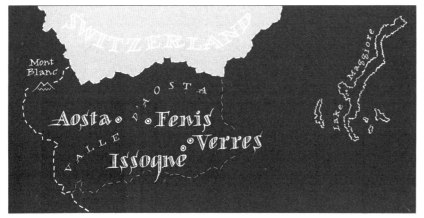

HOTELS

These hotels in the center of town
offer first-rate comforts.

Pavillion. Strada Regionale 60.
0165/842420 (F+)

Royal e Golf. Via Roma 86.
0165/843621 (F+)

RESTAURANTS

French cooking has influenced Valdostana cuisine and menus are often in French as well as Italian. Locally made fontina cheese flavors everything from pasta to veal. Antipastos are extensive and often a meal in themselves.

La Brenva (hamlet of Entreves).
0165/89285 (M)
Camin. Via dei Bagni (hamlet of Larzey). 0165/841497 (E)
La Clotze (hamlet of Planpincieux).
0165/89928 (M)
La Maison de Filippo (hamlet of Entreves). 0165/89968 (M)
Le Vieux Pommier. Piazzale Monte
Bianco 25. 0165/842281 (M)

Pastry Shops and Cafés

The Glarey Caprice, Caffè della Posta, and Le Prive on the Via Roma, and La Main Rose, Via Marconi, are perfect for a relaxing coffee after a day on the slopes.

SKI INFORMATION

Contact the Scuola di Sci Monte
Bianco, Strada Regionale 40,
0165/842477, for private lessons; the Società delle Guide, Piazza A. Henry, 0165/842064, for guides for the difficult runs of La Vallee Blanche and the Toula Glacier. The Azienda di Soggiorno, Piazzale Monte Bianco, 0165/840260, provides information about the wide range of downhill runs and cross-country runs in the area.

EXCURSIONS
The Castles of the Valle d'Aosta

See map, above. One day by car,
25 km. from Issogne.

1. Castello de Issogne. Late-15th century. 0125/929373
2. Castello de Verres. Late-14th century. 0125/929067
3. Castello de Fenis. Mid-14th century. 0165/764263

Castles open 9:30–12:00, 14:00–16:00 or 16:30.

SHOPPING

Courmayeur's market is held every Wednesday in the Piazzale Val Veny, Entreves. Many hand-carved wood decorative objects are on display.

Antiques

Ettore Guichardez
Via Roma 51

Papier Antique
Via Roma 89

Fabrics

Aosta (about ½ hour by car from Courmayeur): L'Erba Voglio
Via Porta Pretoria 14

THE LAKES

Como

HOTELS

Lake Como is noted for its grand hotels offering old-world style and contemporary comforts. The hotels listed below all have pools and lakefront locations, with the exception of Castello di Pomerio, a restored 12th-century castle about 14 km. from Como. Grand Hotel Villa d'Este is surrounded by lavish gardens and has extensive sports facilities.

BELLAGIO: Grand Hotel Villa Serbelloni. 031/950216 (L)
CERNOBBIO: Grand Hotel Villa d'Este. Via Regina 33/B.
031/511471 (L)
MENAGGIO: Grand Hotel Victoria.
Lungo Lago Castelli. 0344/32003 (F)
POMERIO D'ERBA: Castello di Pomerio. Via Como 5. 031/611516 (F)

TREMEZZO: Albergo Grand Hotel
Tremezzo. 0344/40446 (F)

RESTAURANTS

Along with fresh fish from the lake, dishes from Lombardy are the mainstays of dining in Como.

BELLAGIO: Albergo Ristorante la Pergola (hamlet of Pescallo).
031/950263 (M)
Ristorante Grand Hotel. Villa Serbelloni. 031/950216 (E)
CERNOBBIO: Harry's Bar. Piazza Risorgimento 2. 031/512471 (M)
COMO: Navedano. Via Pannilani.
031/261080 (M)
Taverna Blu. Via Puricelli 1.
0341/55107 (M)
ISOLA COMACINA: Ristorante Locanda dell'Isola. 0344/55083 (M)
MOLTRASIO: Albergo Ristorante Caramazza. Via Besana 46.
031/290050 (M)

TREMEZZO: Ristorante al Veluu (hamlet of Rogaro). 0344/40510 (M) Trattoria La Fagurida (hamlet of Rogaro). 0344/40676 (M)

Pastry Shops and Tea Rooms
Comaschi love teatime as much as the English. Pasticcerie Monti, Ferrari, and Franzi in the center of the town of Como are worth a visit. Ask for the local variety of *panettone,* called *resta,* or *mataloc,* a pie with candied fruits.

EXCURSIONS
The Villas of Lake Como
See map, page 268. Grand classical villas, colorful and elegant formal gardens. Magnificent lake views. Allow half day per villa. Travel by car from Como to Tremezzo (about 30 km.). Frequent ferries connect Menaggio, 5 km. north of Villa Carlotta, with Varenna and Bellagio.

It is a good idea to check with Ente Provinciale per il Turismo, Piazza Cavour 17, 031/262091 to confirm days and times that the villas are open to the public.
1. Villa Olmo. Como. Open year-round.
2. Villa Passalacqua. Moltrasio. Open Thursdays, year-round.
3. Villa Balbianello. Lenno. Open Tuesdays from Easter to October. Accessible only by boat from Lenno.
4. Villa Carlotta. Tremezzo. Every day March–October.
5. Villa Monastero. Varenna. Every day April–October
6. Villa Cipressi. Varenna. Every day June–October.
7. Villa Melzi d'Eril. Bellagio. March–October. Check days.
8. Villa Serbelloni. Bellagio. March–October. Check days.

SHOPPING
There are several well-known markets in the Lake Como area, including a silk market along the Via Volta in the Porta Torre section every Saturday, and an antiques fair the first Saturday of every month in the Piazza San Fedele.

Listed below are shops where visitors will find items for the home.

Antiques
Motta Carlo & Figli Restauri
Via Virgilio 28, Cantu. 031/703297

La Soffitta di Adriano Martini
Via Regina 37, Cernobbio.
031/510182

Vanossi Antiquario
Strada dello Spluga, Madesimo (hamlet of Isolato). 0343/510182

Vecchio Arredo di R. Dotti
Via Ponte Nuovo, Cernobbio.
031/512242

Verga Antiquario
Via Volta 54, Como

Bed and Bath
(plain and embroidered bed linens and bath accessories, quilts)

Frette
Via Visconti di Modrone 5
Milan

Pratesi
Via Montenapoleone 21
Milan

Fabrics
Many major silk manufacturers have outlets where a wide range of their fabrics for interior furnishings and clothing can be purchased at close to wholesale prices. (Closed Sundays and Monday mornings.)

Centro della Seta (Mantero)
Via Volta 64. 031/258111

Martinetti
Via Torriani 41. 031/269053

Ratti
Villa Sucota, Via per Cernobbio 19.
031/233111

MILAN

Retail stores with furnishing fabrics.

Etro Accessori
Via Bigli 10

Etro Home Collection
Via Pontaccio 17
Antique and contemporary paisley patterned fabrics, quilts, and pillows.

Naj-Oleari
Via Filefo 5
Bright and lively patterned fabrics, pillows, umbrellas, fabric-covered notebooks.

Rovati
Via Montenapoleone 8
Silks, damasks, brocades.

Wrought Iron
(decorative objects of wrought iron for the interior and exterior)

Penone & Fratelli Borghi
Via Bernini 8/A. 031/787289

Sampietro s.n.c.
Via Volta 21. 031/268160

Maggiore
HOTELS
Like those of Lake Como, the hotels of Lake Maggiore are majestic and renowned for their unique combination of traditional elegance and modern luxury. Each of the hotels listed below has a commanding view of the lake and pools for swimming.
STRESA: Hotel des Iles Borromees. Corso Umberto I, 67. 0323/30431. For reservations in the US, call the CIGA hotels office 1-800-221-2340. Centro Benessere for weight loss, exercise programs, beauty and fitness treatments (L)
Regina Palace. Lungolago Umberto 1, 27. 0323/30171 (F)

RESTAURANTS
Restaurants along the lake primarily serve Lombard and Piedmontese dishes and freshly caught fish.
ARONA: Taverna del Pittore. Piazza del Popolo, 39. 0322/3366 (M)
LESA (NOVARA): Al Camino. Via per Comnago. 0322/7471 (M)
STRESA: L'Emiliano. Corso Italia 48. 0323/31396 (E)
VARESE: Lago Maggiore. Via Carrobbio 19. 0332/231183 (M–E)

EXCURSIONS
The Borromeos' Lake Maggiore
See map, page 268. Princely family's possessions.

Allow half day per island and for the Rocca d'Angera. You can travel to the Borromean islands by boat from Stresa as there is frequent ferry service. Hydrofoil service connects Stresa to the Rocca d'Angera (approximately 50 minutes).
1. Stresa. Depart by boat for Borromean islands.
2. Isola Bella. Baroque palace, gardens, and views.
3. Isola dei Pescatori. Rustic fishing island.
4. Isola Madre. 18th-century *palazzo.* Luxuriant botanical gardens.
5. Rocca d'Angera. Medieval fortress/castle. Outstanding views of lower lake.

SHOPPING
No matter what weekend you travel to the village of Besozzo, you'll find an antiques fair in progress. The market in Luino, a small town on Lake Maggiore's eastern shore, near Switzerland, is the most popular in the region. The wide assortment of merchandise, clothing, ceramics, and cheese and wine regularly attracts shoppers from Switzerland, France, and local towns.

Listed below are shops that sell items for the home.

Antiques
Cose Belle
Corso Marconi 75, Arona

Pasini
Castelletto Ticino

Piccole Cose
Via Labiena, Laveno

THE MEDITERRANEAN
The Italian Riviera

HOTELS

The Splendido is the grand hotel of the Riviera and has been a favorite of European royalty for years. The Cenobio dei Dogi and Paraggi are small inns and have a loyal clientele, so it is important to book rooms for the summer months well in advance. With the exception of the Splendido, all the hotels have waterfront locations and private beaches. The Splendido has its own pool.

CAMOGLI: Cenobio dei Dogi. 0185/770041 (F)
PARAGGI: Paraggi Hotel. 0185/89961 (M)
PORTOFINO: Splendido. 0185/69551 (L)
SANTA MARGHERITA LIGURE: Grand Hotel Miramare. 0185/87014 (F)

RESTAURANTS

Try Vento Ariel and Paraggi for fish, Pitosforo for the *zuppa di pesce* (fish soup), swordfish at Navicello, and lasagne with pesto at Da Puny.

CAMOGLI: Vento Ariel. 0185/771080 (M)
PARAGGI: Paraggi. 0185/89961 (I–M)
PORTOFINO: Da Puny. Piazzetta di Portofino. 0185/69037 (M)
Hostaria da 'O' Batti. Vico Nuovo. 0185/69379 (M)
Navicello. Piazzeta di Portofino. 0185/69471 (M)
Pitosfero. Molo Umberto I. 0185/69020 (M)
Tripoli. Piazza di Portofino. 0185/69011 (M)
SANTA MARGHERITA LIGURE: Trattoria Cesarina. Via Mameli 2/C. 0185/86059 (M).

Pastry Shops, Cafés, Bars

The Gritta (Lungomare), Scafandro (Piazza Centrale), and DeFitta (Piazza Matteotti) in Camogli are good places to go for late-afternoon drinks and snacks. La Gritta in Portofino harbor is a lively predinner watering hole.

EXCURSIONS
Romantic Coastlines: Fishing Villages/Seaside Towns/Splendid Views

See map, page 269. Allow 2–5 days for 100 km. trip. Start in the Riviera town of Nervi, 11 km. from Genoa, and travel by car along the ancient Roman Via Aurelia to Sestri Levante. You may want to leave your car in Sestri Levante and travel by train to the Cinque Terre, as the roads to Monterosso al Mare, the first of the Cinque Terre, are a bit precarious. Local trains on the Genoa–La Spezia route run every hour or two during the day and stop in each of the five villages.

1. Camogli. Boat trips to Punta Chiappa and San Fruttuoso.
2. Santa Margherita Ligure
3. Paraggi
4. Portofino
5. Rapallo
6. Sestri Levante
7. Cinque Terre (five towns of Monterosso al Mare, Vernazza, Corniglia, Manarola, Riomaggiore)

SHOPPING

Look for fine lace at weekly markets in Portofino, Rapallo, and Santa Margherita Ligure, handwoven velvets in Zoagli, straw and raffia bags and hats in most every seaside town. Regional handicrafts can be found in local *botteghe.*

Antiques

Pisani Antiquario
Via Roma 29
Portofino. 0185/69494

Il Balbiano
Via T. Bottaro 28/A
Santa Margherita Ligure. 0185/280597

Fabrics, Embroidery, and Laces

Bottega Famiglia de Martini
Via Scaletta 78
Chiarvari (hamlet of Lorsica)
Hand-loomed damask and linen.

Antica Ditta Attilio Venerose
Via Luccoli 31
Piazza Fontane Maiose
Genoa 010/207447
Lavish fabrics, laces, bedspreads.

The Amalfi Coast

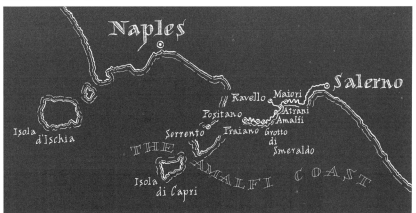

HOTELS

Hotels along the Amalfi Drive are usually situated on hillsides to take advantage of the sea views. Most have swimming pools or access to beaches.
POSITANO: Le Sirenuse. 089/875066 (L)
Royal. 089/875000 (F)
San Pietro. 089/875455 (L)
RAVELLO: Palumbo. 089/857244 (M)

RESTAURANTS

Restaurants by the sea in Italy feature a wide variety of fresh fish, fish chowders, seafood antipastos, and flavorful pastas. Positano's Buca di Bacco is located on the beach, Chez Black is known for its pizzas and a celebrity clientele. The *crespoline* and gnocchi are recommended at Da Salvatore.

AMALFI: Pizzeria Il Mulino. Via Cartiere 34. 089/872223 (I-M)
Rendez-vous. 089/872755 (M)
CONCA DEI MARINI: Conca Azzurra. Piazzale Grotta. 089/871141 (M)
POSITANO: Buca di Bacco. 089/875699 (M)
Chez Black. 089/875036 (M)
Le Tre Sorelle. 089/875452 (M)
RAVELLO: Da Salvatore. Strada Panoramica per Chiusi. 089/857227.

EXCURSIONS
Romantic Coastlines: Fishing Villages/Seaside Towns/Splendid Views

See map, above. Amalfi coast. Start in Positano. Travel by car and allow 1–2 days for the approximately 70 km. trip along the Amalfi Drive (the Lungomare or road nearest the sea). To reach Ravello, perched on the Dragon Hill mountain, one must leave the Lungomare and travel the scenic, sometimes harrowing mountain road that departs from Atrani.

1. Positano (stop at Positano Belvedere for views)
2. Praiano (for boat trip to Grotta di Smeraldo, 15 minutes)
3. Amalfi
4. Atrani
5. Ravello
6. Maiori
7. Salerno

SHOPPING

Once a week most towns along the Amalfi coast have a market day when everything from clothing to fresh local produce can be purchased. Certain towns specialize in various handicrafts, which are diplayed in local *botteghe.* Look for fanciful decorated ceramics, majolica, tiles, and vases in Vietri, near Salerno.

Antiques

Bric à Brac
Piazza Vescovado
Ravello. 089/857153

Le Myricae
Via Colombo 27
Positano. 089/875882

Ceramics and Tiles

Ceramica Artistica Amalfitana
Via Lama della Zecca
Amalfi. 089/872645
Regional patterns.

De Maio Ceramiche Salerno
Via Nazionale 5
Nocera Superiore (Salerno). 081/931011
Hand-crafted tiles, antique and regional patterns made-to-order.

Fabrics, Embroidery, and Laces

Cosi Firenze (De Martino)
26 Via SS Martiri
Salernitani (Salerno). 089/233734
Locally embroidered fabrics.

M. Attanasio
7 Via Ginestre
Salerno. 089/359507
Locally embroidered fabrics.

Tisseranderie
Corso Garibaldi 146/C
Salerno. 089/227853
Fabrics and rugs.

Sardinia

HOTELS

The Cala di Volpe, designed by
Jacques Couëlle to resemble a Moorish
village, and the Pitrizza, architect
Luigi Vietti's stone and terra-cotta
complex of private bungalows, are the
Costa Smeralda's best-known hotels.
The Cervo, in the heart of the Porto
Cervo village, and the Luci di la Mun-
tagna, on a hillside overlooking the
harbor, are stylish and quite reason-
able.
PORTO CERVO: Cala di Volpe.
0789/96083 (L)
Cervo. 0789/96083 (F)
Luci di la Muntagna. 0789/92051 (M)
Pitrizza. 0789/92000 (F+)
Romazzino. 0789/96020 (F)

RESTAURANTS

Many of the hotel restaurants serve a
sophisticated international cuisine.
The poolside luncheon at the Cala di
Volpe Hotel attracts a chic crowd.
Lunch or dinner at the Sporting Club
is also good for people watching.
PORTO CERVO: Cala di Volpe
Hotel. 0789/96083 (M–E)
La Fattoria. 0789/92214 (M)
Grill Hotel Cervo. 0789/92003 (M–E)
Il Pescatore. 0789/92296 (M)
Il Pomodoro. 0789/92007 (I)
Petronilla. 0789/92137 (M)
Pitrizza. 0789/92000 (M–E)
PORTO ROTONDO: Sporting Club.
0789/34005 (E)

Cafés, Clubs

The Portico, the Pub, and the Cervo
Tennis Club are favorite meeting spots
in the center of Porto Cervo. In Porto
Rotondo the cafés in the Piazza San
Marco and Piazzetta di Rudalza are
popular.

SHOPPING

Along the Costa Smeralda in Porto
Cervo and in Porto Rotondo well-
known boutiques of major designers
abound. You have to travel to the
small towns like Castelsardo for hand-
loomed carpets, Bosa for embroidered
fabrics, Nuoro for needlecrafts, Dorgali
for terra-cotta items. The *botteghe* in
each town always offer interesting local
handicrafts.

Antiques

Costo Romano
Casa 146 Rudalza
Porto Rotondo. 0789/34295

Ceramics and Tiles

Cerasarda
Strada Statale per Palau
Olbia. 0789/50264
Contemporary designs.

La Passeggiata
Porto Cervo
Sardinian and contemporary patterns.

Fabrics, Embroidery, and Laces

Loche, Rachele and Angela
Porto Cervo. 0789/92156
Sardinian handcrafted bedspreads,
fabrics, laces.

Sardinia Overseas
Via Sanna Randaccio 36
Cagliari. 070/308346
Southern Sardinian wholesaler of local
bedspreads, curtains, cushions, fabrics,
rugs, and tapestries.

UNITED KINGDOM SOURCE LIST

The following list of shops in Britain is
intended as a general guide to where
you may obtain original Italian provincial furniture and interior furnishings,
such as fabrics, tiles and wrought
ironwork. Further information can be
found in *The British Art & Antiques
Directory*, published by *The Antique
Collector*, National Magazine House,
73 Broadwick Street, London
W1Y 2BP, 01-439 7144. The auction
houses Sotheby's (01-493 8080),
Christie's (01-581 2231) and Bonham's
(01-351 1380) hold regular sales of old
and new *objets d'arts*.

Also included are shops selling contemporary furnishings which will
complement the Italian country style.
For information on individual design-
ers/makers contact the Crafts Council,
Information Section, 12 Waterloo

Place, London SW1, 01-930 4811. (A
free map is available of selected shops
and galleries throughout England.)

For information on shops in your area
selling specific Italian pieces, contact
the Italian Trade Centre, 37 Sackville
Street, London W1, 01-734 2412.

The listings are accurate on going to
press, but subject to change.

ANTIQUES

London

Alexander & Berendt
1A Davies Street
London W1Y 1LL
499 4775
Fine 17th- and 18th-C
Continental furniture
and works of art.

Claude Bornoff
20 Chepstow Corner
Pembridge Villas
London W2
229 8947
Continental porcelain and
furniture.

Brisigotti Antiques
44 Duke Street
London SW1Y 6DD
839 4441
16th- and 18th-C Italian
furniture.

Tony Bunzl & Zal Davar
344 King's Road, London SW3
352 3697
17th- and 18th-C Continental
furniture.

Coexistence
Hobhouse Court
13 Whitcomb Street
London WC2H 7HA
839 6620 *and*
17 Canonbury Lane, London N1 2AS
226 8382
Country furniture and textiles.

Arthur Davidson
78–79 Jermyn Street
London SW1Y 6NB
930 6687/4643
Fine Italian *objets d'arts* from
16th–18th C; furniture, rare
metalwork.

Charles Ede
37 Brook Street, London W1Y 1AJ
493 4944
Roman and Greek antiquities
from Italy.

Gray's Antique Market
58 Davies Street
London W1Y 1LB
629 7034

Guinevere Antiques
578 King's Road, London SW6
736 2917
Antique and decorative furniture.

Jonathan Harris
54 Kensington Church Street
London W8
937 3133
Selected fine-quality European
furniture and works of art,
including tapestries and ceramics.

Heritage Antiques
112 Islington Passage, London N1
226 7789
Specialist in antique metals and
country furniture.

Hollywood Road Antiques
1a Hollywood Road, London SW10
352 5248
Country furniture, decorative
antiques and quilts.

Mallett at Bourdon House
2 Davies Street, Berkeley Square
London W1Y 1LJ
629 2444
Specialists in Continental provincial
and painted furniture; antique garden
statuary.

G. Sarti Antiques
186 Westbourne Grove
London W11 2HR
221 7186
15th–18th C Italian furniture
and marble sculptures.

Jacob Stodel Antiques
116 Kensington Church Street
London W8 4BH
221 2652
European furniture, works of art,
pottery and porcelain to the 18th C.

Robert Young Antiques
68 Battersea Bridge Road
London SW11
228 7847
Country furniture, European folk
art and objects

Regions

A & F Partners
20 London Street
Faringdon, Oxfordshire SN7 7AA
0367 20078
17th–19th C European furniture,
oak, walnut and mahogany.

Simon Brett
Creswyke House, High Street
Moreton-in-Marsh
Gloucestershire GL56 0LH
0608 50751
17th–early 19th C Continental
furniture and works of art.

Cedar Antiques
High Street, Hartley Wintney
Hampshire
025 126 3252
Specialists in fine country furniture.

Annarella Clark Antiques
11 Park Street, Stow-on-the-Wold
Gloucestershire
Painted and country furniture, quilts
and decorative items.

Christopher Clarke
The Fosse Way
Stow-on-the-Wold
Gloucestershire GL54 1JS
0451 30476
18th- and 19th-C Continental
furniture and works of art.

Cottage Antiques
3 Devonshire Place
Skipton Road, Harrogate
N. Yorkshire
0423 68195
Country furniture, domestic cast iron.

George & Helen Gardiner
105 West Regent Street
Glasgow G2 2BA
041 332 1364
Antiques and decorative objects,
tapestries, country furniture,
unusual smart and topical items.

The Granary Galleries
Court House, Ash Priors
near Bishops Lydeard
Taunton, Somerset
0823 432402
Large stock of Continental furniture,
country oak and pine, general antiques.

A. Halsey Antiques
Boffins Boft
Bowcombe Creek
Kingsbridge, Devon
0548 2440
Important stock of 17th- and 18th-C
Continental oak and fruitwood
furniture and works of art.

Jadis
The Old Bank
17 Walcot Buildings, London Road
Bath, Avon
0225 338797
Continental country furniture,
decorative items and painted
furniture.

Richard and Pamela Nadin
12 Paul Street
Frome, Somerset BA11 1DT
0373 64957 and
5 Woolley Street
Bradford-on-Avon,
Wiltshire BA15 1AD
022 16 2476
Unusual decorations and furniture,
folk and primitive art, painted furniture.

Summers, Davis & Son
Calleva House, 6 High Street
Wallingford, Oxfordshire OX10 0BP
0491 36284
Continental decorative furniture
and objects, 17th–19th C.

Tetbury Antiques
39A Long Street
Tetbury, Gloucestershire
0666 52748
17th- and 18th-C Continental
country furniture.

Woburn Abbey Antiques Centre
Woburn Abbey, Woburn,
Bedfordshire MK43 0TP
052 525 350
Fifty shops stocking a variety of
antiques, including porcelain and
painted furniture.

FABRICS AND WALLCOVERINGS

London

The Antique Textile Company
100 Portland Road
London W11
221 7730
Interesting textiles, mostly
pre-1880, of all kinds.

Blanchards Furnishing
173 Sloane Street
London SW1X 9QL
235 6612
Wide range of Italian fabrics.

Jane Churchill
137 Sloane Street
London SW1X 9AY
Bed linen, furnishing fabrics, wallpapers.

Colefax & Fowler
39 Brook Street
London W1Y 2JE
493 2231
Fabrics and wallpapers based
on 18th- and 19th-C designs.

Collier and Campbell
41 Old Town, London SW4
720 7862
Furnishings fabrics and bed linens.

Designers Guild
277 King's Road
London SW3 5EN
370 5001
Country designs in cottons,
wallpapers, curtains, tablecloths
and hand-painted silks.

Elizabeth Eaton
25a Basil Street
London SW3 1BB
589 0118
Continental fabrics and wallpapers.

Frette
98 New Bond Street
London W1Y 9LF
629 5517 and
84 Brompton Road, London SW3
589 4630
Exclusive range of Italian linens.

Liberty & Co.
210–220 Regent Street
London W1 6AH
734 1234

Liberty's Print Shop
340A King's Road
London SW3 5UR
352 6581

Mary Fox Linton
249 Fulham Road
London SW3 6HY
351 0273
Fabrics, wallpapers, furniture.

Lunn Antiques
86 New King's Road
London SW6 4LU
736 4638
Antique textiles, lacework,
embroidery, linens.

Osborne & Little
304 King's Road
London SW3 5UH
352 1456
Fabrics and wallpapers: recent
collection – 'Romagna', reflecting
Medieval and Renaissance pageantry
and the coloring of the mosaics in
St Marks, Venice.

Timney Fowler
388 King's Road
London SW3
351 6562
Fabrics, wallpapers: bold,
monochrome designs.

Warner & Sons
7–11 Noel Street
London W1V 4AL
439 2411
Reproduction historical furnishing
fabrics and wallpapers.

Woodward
20 Heath Street
London NW3 6TE
435 8876
Fabrics and wallpapers, including
Italian pastels.

Regions

G.P. & J. Baker
West End Road, High Wycombe
Buckinghamshire HR11 2QD
0494 33422
London showroom – 18 Berners Street
London W1P 4JA
Quality linens, cottons, wallpaper.

Baileys
73 Warwick Street
Leamington Spa
Warwickshire CV32 4RS
0926 25423
Selection of Italian linens and
bedspreads to order.

Hines of Oxford
2 Addison Drive
Littlemore, Oxford OX4 3UD
0865 776362
Wide range of woven wall-hangings and
tapestries, including tapestries from Italy.

The Honiton Lace Shop
44 High Street, Honiton, Devon
0404 2416
Antique lace, linens, European textiles.

Monkwell
10–12 Wharfdale Road
Bournemouth, Dorset
0202 762456
Furnishing fabrics.

Straight Lace
9 High Street
East Linton, Lothian, Scotland
0620 860017
Antique lace, linen, tiles.

CERAMICS/TERRACOTTA/ STONE
(Interior and exterior)

London

Bibendum
81 Fulham Road
London SW3
581 5817 and
Conran
77–79 Fulham Road
London SW3 6RE
589 7401
Extensive range of Italian
kitchenware and cookware.

The Colonnades
5a Clifton Villas
London W9
402 9834
Variety of stone statues and Italian
terracotta pots.

Delomosne & Son
4 Campden Hill Road
London W8 7DU
937 1804
18th- and 19th-C European pottery,
porcelain and glass.

Divertimenti
68–72 Marylebone Lane
London W1M 5FF
935 0689 and
139 Fulham Road
London SW3 6SD
581 8065
Italian china, glass and tableware;
hand-painted Italian pottery.

Garden Crafts
158 King's Road
London SW6 4LZ
736 1615
Excellent collection of Classical
statues, vases etc., made in cast
stone, marble and terracotta.

Graham & Green
4 and 7 Elgin Crescent
London W11 2HX
727 4594
Wide range of ceramics and glassware.

Habitat
206–222 King's Road
London SW3 5XP
351 1211
(Catalogue for sale, listing branches)
Selected Italian glassware, cookware
and terracotta goods.

Harrods
Knightsbridge
London SW1X 7XL
730 1234

David Mellor
4 Sloane Square
London SW1W 8EE
730 4259 and
26 James Street
London WC2E 8PA
379 6947
Range of cookware, cutlery and glass.

Regions

The Olive Tree Trading Co.
Twickenham Trading Estate
Twickenham
01-892 8031
Specialist importers of a complete
range of plain and decorated
terracotta pots from Italy.

Architectural Heritage of Cheltenham
Boddington Manor, Boddington
Near Cheltenham, Gloucestershire
0242 68741
18th- and 19th-C figures available
from a complete selection of period
garden statuary, including antique
stone and marble pieces.

Andrew Dando
4 Wood Street
Bath, Avon BA1 2JQ
0225 22702
Large stock of porcelain and pottery
(18th- and early 19th-C Continental)

Jenners
40 Princes Street
Edinburgh EH2 2YJ
031 225 2442
Extensive range of china,
kitchenware and tableware.

TILES

London

Carvall Group Ceramics
Norman Road
Rangemoor Industrial Estate
London N15 4NE
801 5331 and
Unit 1
Laurence Trading Estate
Blackwall Lane
Greenwich
London SE10 0AR
Italian hand-painted tiles.

Castelnau Tiles
175 Church Road
London SW13
748 9042

Ceramica Tile Centre
794 Fulham Road
London SW6 5SL
736 7251
Specialists in Italian ceramic,
mosaic and marble floor and wall tiles.

Cornwise
168 Old Brompton Road
London SW5 0BA
373 6890
Wide range of Italian ceramic tiles.

Domus
260 Brompton Road
London SW3 2AS
589 9457
Exclusive range of ceramic
floor and wall tiles, including
terracotta and granite.

Elon Tiles
8 Clarendon Road
London W11 4AP
727 0884
Selection of ceramics, stone and
glazed terracotta floor and wall tiles.

Fired Earth
102 Portland Road
London W11
221 4825
Terracotta and quarry tiles.

W.E. Grant
399–400 Geffrye Street
London E2
729 3380/7332
One of Europe's biggest marble yards.

Langley London
161–167 Borough High Street
London SE1 1HU
407 4444
Range of floor and wall tiles,
including hexagonal terracotta
floor tiles.

Roman Tiles
London House
380 Lea Bridge Road
London E10
556 0904
Hand-painted, terracotta, marble tiles.

Tile Mart
151 Great Portland Street
London W1
580 3814 and
107 Pimlico Road, London SW1
730 7278

Tiles, Tiles, Tiles
168 Old Brompton Road
London SW5
373 6890

Townsends
1 Church Street
London NW8
724 3746
Antiques, tiles in majolica glaze.

Regions

Art Marbles, Stone and Mosaic
Dawson Road
Kingston-upon-Thames
Surrey KT1 3AX
01-546 2023
Marble, granite and slate flooring.

Ceramique Internationale
1 Royds Lane, Wortley Ring Road
Leeds
0532 795031

Fired Earth
Middle Aston, Oxon OX5 3PX
0869 40724
Terracotta and quarry tiles.

The Thomas Group
38 Higher Road
Urmston, Manchester M31 1AP
061 748 2146
Italian marble and granite tiles.

Tile and Wall Finds
46 Enborne Road
Newbury, Berks
0635 49779
Terracotta tiles.

WROUGHT IRON

London

Judy Cole & Son
28 Camden Passage, London N1
226 4539 and
The House of Steel
400 Caledonian Road
London N1
607 5889
Restoration/manufacture and sale
of salvaged originals and reproductions of staircases, balconies, gates,
fireplaces.

Fortress
23 Canonbury Lane, London N1
359 5875
Period stoneware and iron work.

Regions

Artistic Ironworkers Supplies
Unit 1, Whitehouse Road
Kidderminster, Worcestershire
DY10 1HT
0562 753483
Sole distributor of mass-produced
Italian wrought-iron components.

Britannia Architectural Metalwork
5 Normandy Street, Alton
Hampshire GU34 1DD
0420 84427
Architectural metalwork, including
railings, balustrades, grilles and brackets.

For further information on
individual blacksmiths in your
area, contact the British Artists
Blacksmiths Association, Makins,
Whiteway, Stroud, Gloucestershire
GL6 7ER, 028 582366, and also the
Council for Small Industries in
Rural Areas (COSIRA), 141 Castle
Street, Salisbury, Wiltshire SP1 3TB,
0722 336255. To view a range of work,
visit The Fire and Iron Gallery,
Rowhurst Forge, Oxshott Road,
Leatherhead, Surrey, 0372 375148.

Index